LET'S GET VISIBLE
How To Get Noticed And Sell More Books

David Gaughran is the author of *If You Go Into The Woods, Transfection, A Storm Hits Valparaiso* and the best-selling, award-winning *Let's Get Digital: How To Self-Publish, And Why You Should*. Born in Dublin, he currently lives in London, but spends most of his time traveling the world, collecting stories.

Praise for *Let's Get Visible:*
How To Get Noticed And Sell More Books:

"*Let's Get Visible* is the best tool I have discovered for a writer to push sales and visibility to the next level, and an indispensable addition to the library of any indie writer. If you're an indie writer and you're not buying this book, you simply aren't playing this game to win."—Michael Wallace, bestselling author of *The Righteous*.

"Gaughran distills complex subject matter and explains it in a way that anybody can easily understand, and takes the guesswork out of promotion at Amazon. He removes the mysticism and gets you as close as anyone outside of Amazon will probably be to understanding how stuff works behind the curtain."—David Wright, bestselling author of *Yesterday's Gone*.

LET'S GET VISIBLE

DAVID GAUGHRAN

LET'S GET VISIBLE
How To Get Noticed And Sell More Books
ISBN-13: 978-1490310411
ISBN-10: 149031041X

Editor: Karin Cox
Cover Design: Kate Gaughran
Print Formatting: Heather Adkins

E-book edition published May 2013
Print edition published September 2013

This first paperback edition was printed by Createspace

ArribaArribaBooks.com
DavidGaughran.com

Contents

PART IV: ADVERTISING

PART V: LAUNCH STRATEGY

PART VI: SELLING OUTSIDE OF AMAZON

Appendix: Advanced Author Toolkit......................187

Dedication

To the semaphore of yore.

Introduction

In my book *Let's Get Digital: How To Self-Publish, And Why You Should* I explained how the distribution system for books—previously monopolized by the large publishers—was blown apart by the digital revolution. As many of you will have already discovered, the open nature of digital distribution can be a double-edged sword; there are more than 1.5 million e-books in the Kindle Store, with new titles being uploaded every day, around the clock. When anyone can publish a book, the floodgates open.

As such, getting *your* books noticed can be a huge challenge. Even when it seems as if you have cracked the code, and sales are trucking along nicely, the rug can be pulled out from beneath your feet, and it seems like your work has become invisible again. Visibility isn't just a challenge that must be bested once; it requires continual work. Indeed, probably the biggest complaint authors have in this brave new world is not sales (or the lack thereof) but the constant promotion that eats so much into precious writing time. Barely a day goes by without a blog post touting the next *essential* promotional venue for our work, or the latest social network that we *have to* be active on if we want to get our sales moving. Often, such advice suggests moving into areas that make us feel uncomfortable, such as relentlessly pushing our work on Twitter, or disingenuously making friends on Goodreads only to hit them with the hard sell further down the road.

How do we get noticed without driving ourselves crazy or crossing our own ethical boundaries? How do we make our books visible without spending so much time on promotion that we have nothing left for writing? How can we promote in a cost-effective way (that won't make us go nuts)?

Fear not, fellow writer. *Let's Get Visible* is here to help.

This book will do two things. It will break down Amazon's famous recommendation engine and detail the various opportunities for exposure on Amazon's sites. Plus, it will give you practical help on how to implement this knowledge. By using the tips outlined in this book, you *will* get your book noticed. Whether your book sells or not is up to you. Because if you don't have the basics in place—a striking cover that speaks to your genre, an enticing blurb that draws readers into the book, a sample that grabs them (with clean formatting), and a price that doesn't make them think twice—no amount of visibility will do you any good. If you aren't sure whether you have those basics in place, or you haven't published anything yet, I urge you to read *Let's Get Digital* first, which will cover all of the steps you need to get your book in shape and ready to profit from the visibility that *Let's Get Visible* will help you attain. Considering that a lot of the strategies here aim to place you on various lists on the Amazon site, an appealing, professional cover is particularly important. I can't stress that enough.

Assuming you do have those basics in place, you probably share the same frustrations that many writers have when it comes to the promotional treadmill. Getting your book noticed can seem like an impossible task. Even when you manage to carve out some visibility for your titles, it often seems fleeting, and the sales surge can disappear as quickly as it arrived. Many writers are awkward penguins who don't enjoy promoting their work and are aghast at the notion of becoming the internet equivalent of a door-to-door salesman. That's fine. This book will not urge you to flood Twitter with spammy "buy my book" messages. Nothing in this book will make you penguins squirm. Promise. This book also won't push time-heavy strategies on you. I won't urge you to join Goodreads and spend countless hours reviewing books and forcing yourself on various reader groups. I won't suggest you join teams where you spend hours tweeting about other people's books, which you haven't read, in the hope that they will do the same for you.

None of the strategies outlined in this book will

take up too much time. Indeed, I will urge you to cut back on time-heavy promotional activity and substitute it with something altogether more powerful: knowledge of the algorithms that determine which books receive the spotlight, and ways to exploit that knowledge to your advantage. In short, this book will help you make your books visible, and will free up more time for writing (and the rest of your life).

Some of the tricks are simple: such as having a short note at the back of your books asking readers (nicely) for a review. Doing that led to my review rate tripling overnight. No longer did I have to spend countless hours hounding book reviewers, only to have my novel join the back of an endless queue. Instead, the reviews poured in without any further effort on my part. Another simple suggestion is to set up a mailing list, and to make that link the first thing readers see when they finish your book. Doing that has allowed me to build up a considerable list of readers who will buy my work the second it is released—landing my books high in the charts, gaining them crucial exposure to new readers, and driving further sales.

That's the easy stuff, but not everything in this book is that straightforward. Some of it will require a little work on your part. The inner workings of Amazon aren't always easy to decode. The strategies I outline might, at times, seem strange (such as staggering news of a new release over several days, rather than telling everyone all at once). But there is sound reasoning behind such thinking, and everything is explained in the simplest possible terms with plenty of concrete examples. By the time you have finished this book, you will have a series of different marketing techniques you can apply to all of your titles, depending on their current sales level. You will learn how to choose the right categories (and when to change them), and you will learn what factors actually govern Sales Rank and how the Best Seller & Popularity lists work (and the difference between the two). Once you understand that, you will learn how to maximize free runs, and how to get the most out of a paid advertisement, a group promotion, or a limited-time sale.

Most importantly, you will have divested yourself of time-wasting, frustrating promotional strategies that do nothing other than cost you precious writing time. But before we get to that, we have to deal with the dreaded sales cliff.

The Sales Cliff

All authors know that sales can ebb and flow. Sometimes the reasons are clear, but at other times they are mystifying. A spike in sales after being featured on a major site like Pixel of Ink, Ereader News Today, or BookBub has an obvious explanation: your book is suddenly visible to thousands and thousands of new readers who have never heard of it before. Featured authors can enjoy the afterglow of a resultant spike for the following days or weeks.

What is often less obvious is why sales suddenly collapse. The same book that was riding high in the charts one day suddenly becomes untouchable. It's as if the book has become invisible to readers. If you keep a close eye on your daily sales numbers, you might even notice this phenomenon occurring roughly a month after a big sales day. But what is the cause? Can this trend be reversed? And is there a way to avoid this "sales cliff" altogether?

To answer those questions, you need to understand what feeds into the various algorithms that Amazon and the other retailers use to calculate lists such as Best Sellers and Hot New Releases that are dotted around their sites. Sometimes, these recommendation engines are working in your favor, displaying your book to thousands of potential purchasers. Other times, it's as if your book has been warehoused, and readers never seem to stumble across it. But what if there were a way to get the system to view your book more favorably? What if there were a way to trigger those recommendations for your own titles?

Let's Get Visible attempts to solve a number of problems, but chiefly how to make your book stand out in the endless sea of the Kindle Store. It will explain the ways in which Amazon highlights particular books to readers. It will teach you how to make your book more attractive to the algorithms that determine what books are recommended. And it will show you how to keep the dreaded sales cliff at bay.

But before you can take advantage of the system, you need to understand how it works.

In the first section—*Amazon Algorithms*—you will learn how Sales Rank is calculated, what factors affect it, and what doesn't (despite popular beliefs to the contrary). You will hear about the various lists that present key opportunities for visibility in the Kindle Store, such as the Best Seller lists, Hot New Releases, the Popularity list, and Movers & Shakers. I will also explain how Also Boughts work, and why they are such crucial drivers of sales. Finally, Amazon's email recommendations will be covered, and strategies for qualifying for that killer marketing push will be outlined.

Parts II and III are called *Free Pulsing* and *Price Pulsing*, but don't let those labels intimidate you; they're just fancy terms for dropping your price briefly, or setting your book free for a short time. These sections will be the first chance for you to put this knowledge into practice, so that your books can start getting some visibility. You will get practical promotional tips to help you hit those Best Seller lists, including running a limited time sale or a group promotion, making the most out of KDP Select, free matching, and perma-free.

Part IV is *Advertising,* and it is where you will find out which big reader sites are worth your money and also learn how to evaluate any advertising opportunity to ensure you always get a positive return on your investment. By the end of this section, you will know how to maximize your advertising dollars by estimating potential sales and choosing the correct categories for the promotion. Subjects like post-advertising pricing or category switching will also be covered.

The fifth section, *Launch Strategy*, is where you put all the pieces together to make sure your latest book has the best possible start. It will explain why you should avoid the standard launch procedure of seeking to push your book as high as possible on the first day. It will teach you how to set-up a mailing list, how to drive sign-ups, and how to propel your book onto the Hot New Releases list (which will further grow your sales).

It might seem more natural to place launch strategies at the, start, but this entire book assumes you already have several titles released. If you don't, what follows will be of limited use to you, and your time is probably best spent focusing on new work. The advice in *Let's Get Visible* is ordered to teach you how to boost the visibility of your existing titles, before stitching everything together to show you how to properly launch your next book, staking out that crucial exposure right from the start. It might seem a little counterintuitive to have launch strategies towards the end, but to be frank, if you haven't assimilated what has gone before, launch strategies will be confusing.

Selling Outside Amazon is the final section. Here, the other retailers are covered, primarily focusing on the biggest players: Barnes & Noble, Apple, and Kobo. The visibility challenges are more extreme outside of Amazon, and the reasons are explained in some depth.

Some writers have managed to be successful, however, and their strategies are outlined. You may decide to grant Amazon exclusivity as a result, or at least focus your marketing efforts there, but all options are covered.

Soon, you will have enough knowledge to make decisions with confidence, as part of an overall marketing plan, instead of shooting in the dark. But first you need to understand the Amazon algorithms. If their mere mention causes you brief panic, don't worry. Everything is explained clearly. By the end of the first section you will have an intuitive understanding of how Amazon recommends books to readers, and how you can take advantage of that.

Ready to dive in?

PART I:
AMAZON ALGORITHMS

More experienced or tech-savvy writers may be tempted to skip this section and move straight to the more practical sections on advertising and marketing. I urge you not to do that and to go over these basics first. There are so many myths about how ranking and Best Seller lists work that it's crucial to rid yourself of those before attempting to apply the strategies I outline. If you are unsure how the Popularity list is calculated, for example, or how it discriminates against cheaper books, you might fail to maximize returns from a limited time sale or a free run.

1. *Amazon Sales Rank*

Sales Rank has often been the subject of fevered speculation. Amazon typically remains tight-lipped about the exact algorithm—aside from a general declaration that your Sales Rank reflects how your book is doing *at that moment* in relation to all others—leading some authors to throw their hands up and declare it unknowable. That is a mistake. As for any system, the behavior of Sales Rank algorithms can be observed, and can even follow a clear pattern.

It's actually a lot simpler than many think. When you first publish a book, you won't have a ranking until you get a sale. Once that first purchase filters through the system, you will be assigned a number that reflects how well your book is selling *in relation to all others*, and that number will be updated hourly (although books at the bottom of the rankings may see less frequent updates). #1 is the top-selling book on Amazon, *at that moment*. And #23,459 means that there are *currently* 23,458 books selling better than yours. If you are having trouble finding your Sales Rank, it's noted on the product page of each book, just below the publisher information. You can also view the Sales Rank for all of your titles simultaneously in Author Central (*bit.ly/Visible1*).

While Amazon claims that sales reports are live, there can often be a delay of a few hours before they register in the KDP dashboard, and then it can be another hour (or more) before that transaction affects your Sales Rank. Free downloads can be reported quicker, but free titles have a separate ranking system. When free books revert to the paid listings, those free downloads don't count towards your Sales Rank whatsoever (but do affect other algorithms, which we'll get to). Paid sales take longer to register on the KDP dashboard. In fact, recently Amazon has been batching sales reports, leading to less regular updates. It remains to be seen whether this is a permanent change, or whether it is something that will be resolved at the next update to their reporting systems.

How Is Sales Rank Calculated?

Sales Rank behaves in a logical, predictable way. If your sales increase, your ranking improves (i.e. moves closer to #1). If your sales decrease, or if you stop selling altogether, your ranking worsens. If you have access to your sales reports (i.e. if you're a self-publisher who uploads directly to KDP), you can make reasonably accurate predictions about how your book will shift in the rankings on the next update. As the ranking system is relative, the seasonal nature of the bookselling business plays a part. A burst of 100 sales in a single day will lead to a better ranking on June 26 than it will on December 26, when all of the new Kindle owners will be loading their new devices with e-books. Even so, by looking at the ranking of any given book, you can (roughly) estimate how many they are selling *at that particular moment*.

The only thing that directly affects Sales Rank is sales. Some people think the number of reviews you have influences your Sales Rank. It doesn't, and neither do Likes, tags, free downloads, Also Boughts, clicks, page views, samples downloaded, your book's genre, or anything else. Free downloads can influence your position on the Popularity list (which some people confuse with the Best Seller list), which in turn can drive sales and will then improve your ranking, but they don't *directly* affect Sales Rank. Similarly, having a large number of overwhelmingly positive reviews can help sway a prospective reader who is on the fence about purchasing your book, but it won't *directly* affect Sales Rank.

Finally, a particularly widespread belief is that the price of your book is a factor in Sales Rank. It's not. Like free downloads, price can influence your position on the Popularity List, which can in turn grant you visibility that leads to sales, and which can then improve your Sales Rank, but it doesn't have a *direct* influence on Sales Rank. We'll cover all of that in detail, but for now, you just need to keep one thing clear in your head: **the only thing that *directly* affects Sales Rank is sales**. Most misunderstandings about the Amazon system spring from these myths, so make sure you are clear on that point. (Please note that when an Amazon Prime member borrows a book from the Kindle Owners' Lending Library, that borrow counts as a sale for the purposes of Sales Rank calculations. You will only get such borrows if you are enrolled in KDP Select.)

A believer in the myth that price affects Sales Rank might counter with an example of one book being ranked higher than another, despite the latter selling more. Yes, that can happen, but it's all explained by how different sales are weighted by Amazon's algorithms. For example, more recent sales are weighted most heavily. However, after five days or so, those sales have very little weighting whatsoever. In addition, *velocity* is valued. Selling 20 books in the space of an hour will push you much higher in the rankings than if they were spread over a day (or a week). This led to some authors gaming the system by organizing a group of people to buy their books at the same time. It worked for a while, until Amazon recalibrated the algorithms to push those books down the charts just as quickly as they rose. That development is important, as it now means that brief sales spikes from something like an ad on a reader site no longer lead to as many residual sales afterward. It also affects launch strategy, which we'll get to later in this book.

For now, though, simply know that the only thing that improves your book's Sales Rank is sales. How recent those sales are is important, as is velocity, but it all comes down to sales.

As the ranking system is designed to update hourly, things can change quickly. But if you track any given book over a period of time, you can get a pretty good idea of how well it's doing (a tool like Novelrank or the KND Tracker is helpful here too, and you will find details of those in the *Advanced Author Toolkit* at the back of this book). This is important and will help you estimate how many sales your book needs to make to appear on Best Seller lists or on other Amazon lists. The following chart will help you to roughly estimate sales based on ranking and was crowdsourced by a large group of self-publishers on KBoards, formerly known as KindleBoards (*bit.ly/Visible2*).

Please note that these numbers, and, indeed, this whole discussion, refer to e-books. The print side is very different. When I'm discussing rankings, unless otherwise flagged, I'm referring to the US Kindle Store. Far fewer sales will be needed to achieve any given Sales Rank in the other Kindle Stores.

Rank To Sales Estimator

#1 to #5 = 3,500+ books a day (sometimes a lot more)
#5 to #10 = 2,000–3,500 books a day
#10 to #20 = 1,100–2,000+
#20 to #65 = 850–1,100
#80 = 850

#90 = 750
#275 = 325
#500 = 200
#1000 = 100
#2000 = 50–55
#3000 = 40–45
#4000 = 30
#5000 = 20–25
#7500 = 16
#12000 = 10
#25000 = 5
#32000 = 3
#42500 = 2
#70000 to #100000 = 1
#100,000+ = less than 1 a day

It's important to note that the numbers above refer to the estimated number of sales needed to hold a given ranking. A greater number of sales will be required to attain that rank in the first place (as sales made in the last few days will count *somewhat* towards your current Sales Rank). Please also note that this chart is correct as of May 2013. As the digital market grows, more sales will be needed to hold any particular rank (and even more sales will be needed to hold that rank during busy periods like Christmas). That aside, the above chart will serve as a guideline for estimating how many sales you require to hit the Best Seller list in your categories, as well as other lists such as Hot New Releases—the importance of which is explained in the following chapters.

2. Amazon's Recommendation Engine

There's an old adage that best sellers are chosen rather than made, and there's some truth to that. The amount a publisher splurges on the advance has to be recouped before the book turns a profit. The more money that has to be recouped, the greater the marketing budget. Sleeper hits are the exception for a reason. It's a lot easier to hit the Best Seller lists when your book is on the front table of every single Barnes & Noble than when it is spine-out at the back of a handful of stores (or gathering dust in the warehouse).

It often comes as a surprise to those outside of the publishing industry that these bookstore spots are bought and sold, and that whether a book is face-out or spine-out (or on the front table) is something that tends to be agreed upon in the contract between the publisher and the bookseller. But when you explain the value of this real estate (known as "co-op"), it all makes sense, even if the scales may fall from the uninitiated's eyes a little.

It's very different on Amazon, where a weird

form of meritocracy decides what books are visible, rather than backroom deals with large publishers. While Amazon hasn't done away with "virtual co-op" completely, the benefits of Amazon's automated book recommendation system are available to any title, author, or publisher—provided their titles perform well enough.

Amazon's basic philosophy is simple: it will always (attempt to) show you the book you are most likely to purchase. The system is largely agnostic, meaning that Amazon doesn't care if the featured title is published by you, me, them, or Penguin, and it also doesn't care if the book is 99c or $14.99—it will show you the title you are most likely to purchase.

In simple terms, the system is based on aggregating data about your browsing, purchasing, and reading habits, and then extrapolating what you would like to read next based on all of Amazon's other customers who have similar histories (sadly, we aren't as unique as we'd like to believe). Those recommendations manifest in different ways. One of the crudest iterations is the Also Boughts (that strip of books on the product page of your book to display the other titles customers have purchased along with your *cri de coeur*). At the other end of the scale are the millions of personalized emails Amazon sends out to customers every day to provide tailored purchase recommendations.

A word of warning: don't get too excited if you receive, or a friend receives, an Amazon email recommending one of your books. This *does not* mean you have qualified for a widespread email push, or that sales are about to rain down on you. It's more than likely that you (or your friend) were the only person to receive that email, because such emails are based on browsing habits. You, or your friend, may have been checking your reviews, or your Sales Rank, so the system thought you were a prospective reader on the fence about buying, and it tried to nudge you into purchasing. You have to get quite high in the rankings, and sustain that Sales Rank for a considerable period, before your book will qualify for a widespread email blast.

Back to those emailed recommendations. Some of you may quibble about the quality of the suggestions you receive from Amazon, but you should note that writers especially might get some odd recommendations. Keep in mind that browsing habits play a big part in this. If you are regularly stalking other books to check on their performance, Amazon will likely suggest these to you, along with similar books.

For customers who have more "pure" browsing histories, however, the recommendation engine can be spookily accurate, and it is widely considered to be the best in the e-commerce world (*bit.ly/Visible3*). And, of course, Amazon's recommendation accuracy increases every time you browse, purchase, or read, and with every huge chunk of investment Amazon makes in gathering data and honing its algorithms.

Amazon's accuracy presents quite the challenge for physical bookstores. In a recent post, publishing blogger Passive Guy described it perfectly (*bit.ly/Visible4*):

When a customer walks into a Barnes & Noble store, is it possible for a clerk to be waiting at the door with a selection of books that the customer will probably want to read? This is exactly what happens whenever an Amazon book purchaser visits the Amazon web site. As a matter of fact, Amazon performs the electronic equivalent of rearranging a Barnes & Noble so all the visitor's favorite book types are right at the front of the store.

Of course, Barnes & Noble also has an online store, and Amazon faces additional players in the e-book arena, such as Apple and Kobo. But all of Amazon's online competitors share the same fundamental flaw: the customer experience is considerably poorer. Kobo's search function is terrible. Apple makes it plain difficult to simply browse. And the problems with Barnes & Noble's online store are so extensive that I devoted an entire blog post to them (*bit.ly/Visible5*). Suffice to say that many Barnes & Noble customers find the online store experience so poor that they use Amazon to find the books they wish to read next and then return to Barnes & Noble to purchase them (or to attempt to, in some cases).

While some of the disparity in customer experience is down to lack of investment, simply throwing money at the problem won't close the gap because there are two distinct philosophies at work. It's quite clear that all three of Amazon's primary competitors want to train customer attention on that "virtual co-op"—the prominent positions that large publishers have purchased to hawk their books. I'm sure these retailers make good money from auctioning off these spots, and I'm also sure they are quite pleased that the books they are granting this all-important visibility to are ones priced at $9.99 rather than 99c.

But it's a huge mistake. Explaining why requires a little detour to Silicon Valley.

The reason Google beat out Yahoo is simple: relevance. While Yahoo auctioned off advertising spots to the highest bidder, Google's AdWords made an ad's relevancy (decided by the click-thru rate) a key component in deciding what ads got the prime real estate above search results. Google knew that approach might make them less money in the short term, but it also knew that, over time, users would trust the ads more (i.e. click on them more) if they were more relevant. And we all know what happened next.

I'm sure Amazon was watching that battle, because their recommendation engine takes the same approach: it always shows readers the books they are most likely to purchase, even if that recommendation makes Amazon less money than an alternative. Amazon knows that if its customers trust its recommendations, they will act on them more often (and spend more money). Amazon knows that even if it loses money on an immediate recommendation, it will make more in the long run.

That's why Google won, and it's why Amazon is winning. It's also why self-publishers tend to do much better on Amazon then elsewhere—even relative to Amazon's market share. Self-publishers typically report selling 90% or more of their books on Amazon (even before the advent of KDP Select and exclusivity), despite most observers pegging the Kindle's market share in the US at around 60% to 65%. Self-publishers don't tend to have access to the front tables at Barnes & Noble, either online or in the physical stores. The whole point of those front tables is to draw readers' attention, to intercept them before they start browsing the shelves.

Amazon gives self-publishers a much more level playing field; those all-important opportunities for visibility—those digital front tables—are open to anyone. And because those front tables are displaying the books customers actually want to read, rather than the ones large publishers most want to sell, people buy more books. This simple fact explains the dominance of Amazon, but it also represents a clear threat to large publishers: they aren't just losing control over what books get published, but also over what books get *recommended*.

The opportunity for self-publishers is even clearer. While large publishers are spending their time railing against Amazon, we can crack the code and use the system to our advantage. But to do that, we need to delve a little deeper into this recommendation engine.

Figuring out how the different parts function has a very practical side effect: understanding how to make our books visible.

Starting with Best Seller lists.

3. Best Seller Lists

The most basic components of Amazon's recommendation engine are Best Seller lists. The first thing to note is that the only thing that affects placement on them is your Sales Rank, which, as explained in the last chapter, is based *purely* on sales, tempered by the recency and velocity of same. Some writers believe that placement on Best Seller lists is influenced by reviews or tags or price or genre or other such nonsense, but it's all down to your *current* Sales Rank, which updates hourly if the system isn't affected by delays or glitches, or if you aren't lurking down near the bottom of the rankings where updates can be less frequent.

With that out of the way, the next thing to flag is that Best Seller lists are broken down by categories and subcategories. The top-level Best Seller list is the Kindle Store Top 100 (*bit.ly/Visible7*). This is the Holy Grail. Appearing in the Top 100 can have a huge impact on sales because numerous readers browse it to see what is trending in the charts, so appearing there acts as social proof for prospective purchasers. The Kindle Store (and, by reflection, its Top 100) doesn't just contain e-books but also items like games, magazines, blogs, and newspapers. You will regularly see some of those appearing in the charts, such as a digital subscription to the *New York Times*. The Kindle Store is subdivided into further categories, such as Kindle eBooks, Devices, Accessories, Blogs, Magazines, Newspapers, and Singles. And then the Kindle eBooks category is further divided by genre and subject, all of which contain further subcategories, some of which are quite granular.

Choosing the right category for your book is crucial, and changing it at certain times can be very important. All of that is covered in detail in the next chapter, but for now it's merely important to note that each category and subcategory has its own Top 100, providing you with extra opportunities for visibility.

Some categories get more eyeballs than others. Naturally, a popular category like *Romance* will have more readers browsing it than something a little more niche like *Mystery, Thriller & Suspense > Mysteries > Cat Sleuths* (yes, that really is a category) *(bit.ly/Visible6)*. By clicking on the book ranked #100 in any given category, you can consult the *Rank to Sales Estimator* (which is reprinted in the back of this book in the *Advanced Author Toolkit*), and estimate how many sales you will need to qualify for the respective Best Seller list.

The real action, though, is on the front page of any given Best Seller list (especially for subcategories, as opposed to the Kindle Store Top 100, where many readers actually page through the whole thing). For some bigger categories, like *Mystery, Thriller & Suspense*, you might get a decent amount of readers browsing the second or third pages too, but in general, the first page of any Best Seller list is where you will see a marked difference in sales.

As you browse the Best Seller lists, you may notice a selection of free books alongside the paid listings. At the time of writing, Amazon is experimenting with hiding those free books behind a tab, which will make appearing on the paid side even more valuable (as there are no free books to distract readers); it will also decrease the visibility of those free books. Amazon appears to be doing split testing (hiding the free books to one group of readers but not to others, and then switching). This kind of split testing is quite common. Right now, it's not clear whether this will be permanently implemented (often features are tested and then dropped), but it is something to watch.

Either way, appearing on the Best Seller list for your chosen categories (and, if possible, the first page or two), should be a key part of any marketing strategy and will be outlined later in this book. Don't panic if you write in a very competitive genre. The Best Seller lists aren't the only opportunity for visibility on Amazon, and we will cover all of the others in the following chapters. First of all, though, we need to delve a little deeper into categories so that you can choose the correct ones to maximize visibility for your book, and so that you learn how to change them at the right time.

4. Categories

If you understand how the category system works, you can give your book instant visibility on Amazon. Self-publishers are at a slight disadvantage here. They get to choose only two categories when uploading, whereas traditional publishers, depending on their arrangements with Amazon, can choose up to five. However, many publishers don't understand Amazon's categories and fail to use the system to their advantage. They either don't use all categories available to them or, without drilling down further, they choose something generic like *Fiction*, which is useless as a category unless you are at the very top of the Amazon rankings. Just choosing the right subcategory for your work can give your book a real head start.

Drilling Deep

There are a huge number of books in *Fiction* (over 750,000 at the time of writing). Competition is fierce, and appearing in the Top 100 of *Fiction* requires a tremendous number of sales, which will be beyond most mere mortals. However, choosing *Fiction* as a category is a waste for a much more simple reason: electing a subcategory of *Fiction* will get you into the *Fiction* category as well.

Even if you drill down several levels to choose something like *Kindle Store > Kindle eBooks > Fiction > Mystery, Thriller & Suspense > Thrillers > Political,* your book will still show in all of the top-level categories above the one you have chosen (i.e. *Fiction; Mystery, Thriller & Suspense; Thrillers*). In other words, when you pick something more specific like that, you are multiplying your potential visibility opportunities rather than restricting them. If your book is doing particularly well, you will appear on a number of Top 100 lists, all of which will drive further sales.

By checking the ranking of the books in each subcategory, you will get an idea of how competitive each one is. Using the *Rank to Sales Estimator,* you can estimate whether your book would make the respective Top 100. Wherever possible, it's wise to choose categories in which you can currently compete. Indeed, all other things being equal, it's best to choose a category in which your book will appear on the first couple of pages.

Let me give you a concrete example. Let's say you are a romance writer who normally sells 30 copies per day of a given title. You might have opted for *Romance > Contemporary,* as it seemed a good fit for your book. *Romance > Contemporary* currently requires a Sales Rank of #332 (or around 300 sales a day) to even hit the back of the respective Top 100. But if you opted for *Romance > Inspirational* instead, you would find the competition a little less tough. Qualifying for that Best Seller list requires (at the time of writing) a Sales Rank of #5,325 (or around 20 sales a day). In the case of your book, which is selling 30 copies a day, you wouldn't just hit the Top 100, you'd be sitting pretty at around #65 in the chart, gaining crucial extra eyeballs on your work.

I'll cover this in more detail in *Chapter 8: The Importance of Popularity*, but the Popularity lists will give you an idea of how many books there are in each category. For example, there are currently 618,758 titles in *Literature & Fiction* but only 5,315 titles in *Literature & Fiction > Genre Fiction > War*. Going through the various categories can indicate the relative size of each genre and subgenre, and can also help you identify a category that might provide an easier path to visibility. Be warned, however, that a very small category might not receive a lot of reader traffic. If the lists are small and stagnant, readers may not return to be faced with the same books each time.

Doubling Down

As a self-publisher, you have just two categories to play with. It can be a good approach to pick one competitive category that you occasionally qualify for, and one that is a little less competitive and enables you to always hit the Best Seller list. This way, you have a chance of front-page action in a smaller category, plus you're covered if you have a good run of sales and start moving up the Best Seller list of a more frequently browsed category.

An example might help illustrate this point. If you have written a gritty crime novel set on an army base in Iraq, the obvious category choices might be *Kindle Store > Kindle eBooks > Literature & Fiction > Genre Fiction > Mystery & Thrillers > Crime*, and *Kindle Store > Kindle eBooks > Literature & Fiction > Genre Fiction > Mystery & Thrillers > Police Procedurals*. However, there are two weaknesses to this approach. First of all, they are both very competitive categories, requiring around 100 sales a day to hit even the front page of the Best Seller lists. Second, they are both roots of the same top-level category: *Mystery & Thrillers*. Where possible, it is advantageous to opt for two distinct categories to maximize visibility, which is especially important when sales spike. You could keep *Kindle Store > Kindle eBooks > Literature & Fiction > Genre Fiction > Mystery & Thrillers & Suspense > Crime*, and choose something a little less competitive for the second.

Kindle Store > Kindle eBooks > Literature & Fiction > Genre Fiction > Action & Adventure requires around 200 sales a day to hit the front page of the Best Seller list but others are less demanding such as *War* (50 sales a day), and *Men's Adventure* (40 sales a day). You should attempt to identify a number of such alternative categories for each title, which will give you options when the time comes to switch. When sales improve and your numbers make you eligible for a Best Seller list in a more competitive category (which is invariably one browsed by more readers), you should go for it. If your sales dip, you can switch back to a less competitive category so that you at least have some visibility during a downturn. But waxing and waning sales aren't the only reason to switch categories.

Freshening Up

Sometimes it's a good idea to seek out virgin territory. If you have had a run at the charts in your normal categories, or gained a lot of exposure from a successful free run, changing categories prior to a new promotion can introduce your work to a whole new group of readers.

Monique Martin uses this strategy regularly to great effect. Her *Out of Time* series could be classified as *Time Travel Romance*, *Historical Fiction*, *Historical Romance*, *Historical Fantasy*, *Mystery*, or even *Romantic Suspense* (as it has elements of each and obeys the respective genre conventions). She regularly switches categories from one to the other prior to a free run or an ad spot. This can negate the diminishing returns that writers can sometimes see after repeatedly hitting the same pool of readers. She even places different books in the series in different categories, widening her visibility footprint.

Now, not all books will easily slot into so many different categories. But if this option is open to you and your work, experiment with this approach. Just be careful that your book is a good fit for the categories you are playing with. You don't want to incur the wrath of romance readers because your book doesn't have a happily ever after.

Phantom Cats

Like virtually all e-book retailers, Amazon gives you numerous category choices when uploading your book or making changes. These are based on BISAC subject headings, which are industry standard. However, it's *extremely* important to note that these don't always reflect the actual categories in the Kindle Store.

While the system attempts to map your BISAC choice to a Kindle Store category, it doesn't always work. This leads to the situation where you have:

(a) Categories that appear only in Books (i.e. the print book listings and not in the Kindle Store itself);

(b) International-only categories (for example, Medical Thriller was a category in the UK Kindle Store, but not in the US until Amazon recently added it);

(c) Unique Kindle Store categories that are not selectable when uploading

This inexact mapping between the BISAC-inspired choices in the KDP interface and the actual categories in the Kindle Store creates both a problem and an opportunity.

The problem comes when you select a category that does not exist in the Kindle Store, like *Fiction & Literature > Drama > Latin America*—as I have done in the past. While it exists on the Book side, it doesn't have a corresponding category in the Kindle Store. It's essentially wasting a category choice. Before selecting your categories, you should ensure that your prospective choice actually exists in the Kindle Store itself. This is really important and I can't stress it enough.

But there's an opportunity here too. Those Kindle Store-only categories are sparsely populated as few authors or publishers have chosen them. As there are fewer books to compete with, you don't need to sell very many books to appear in the charts; this gives crucial visibility opportunities to books that aren't selling particularly well, or those that have just been released and haven't built up a head of steam yet.

For example, *Mystery & Thrillers* is one of the most competitive categories in the Kindle Store, second only to *Romance*. Appearing on any *Mystery & Thrillers* list is a serious challenge that requires impressive sales— something that might be beyond most writers until they have several titles out and have built a dedicated following. However, with a little poking around in the subcategories, you can identify some that don't need very many sales at all. *Technothriller* is one, and *Mystery > Series* is another. Neither is selectable from the KDP interface, so there aren't many books in either category.

You only need Sales Rank of #26,483 to hit the Best Seller list for the former, and #27,586 for the latter (or around 5 sales a day), considerably fewer than in other *Mystery & Thriller* categories. If you explore the categories, you will find plenty more.

You might be wondering how to get into these categories if you can't select them from the KDP dashboard. It's pretty simple. First, you must select *Non-Classifiable* as one of your categories, and then you must email KDP through the dashboard with the *full path* of the category you wish to appear in (e.g. *Kindle Store > Kindle eBooks > Literature & Fiction > Genre Fiction > Mystery & Thrillers > Mystery > Series*).

Normally, this process is painless and only takes a couple of days. However, lately I've been hearing reports that KDP are pushing back on letting authors into certain categories (and, indeed, restricting further the choices available from the dashboard). The customer service representatives are mistaken here, and, judging by their replies, seem to be under the impression that authors are trying to gain access to certain controlled categories (such as Kindle Singles). If you get a confusing or incorrect response, you must persist. It may take multiple (frustrating) exchanges, but you will get it resolved eventually—and it's worth it.

I raised this issue with Amazon representatives at the London Book Fair in April 2013. While they didn't seem to be aware of the problem, they did promise to investigate. Hopefully, it will be resolved soon. I also impressed on them the need for further specific subcategories in certain genres, and I hope that progress will be made on that front too.

Before we move on, an earlier caveat must be repeated. It's a bad idea to choose any category that isn't a good fit for your work. The few readers who do download your book will probably be outside your target audience, and they will likely respond with poor reviews. Tread carefully. Nobody likes being hoodwinked.

Childless Cats

In some cases, the above advice is no good because your target category has no subcategories. This can be extremely frustrating, and it's a situation I face with my historical novel *A Storm Hits Valparaiso*.

The natural categories for that book are *Historical Fiction* and *Literary Fiction*. Unfortunately, however, neither of those categories have a subcategory. In the case of *Historical Fiction*, you tend to require a ranking of between #2,500 and #3,000 to even hit the back of the Best Seller list, which is around 40 to 50 sales a day. *Literary Fiction* is even more competitive, and you often need a Sales Rank of between #2,000 and #2,500 to qualify—around 50 to 55 sales a day. Given that *A Storm Hits Valparaiso* rarely sells at that level outside of a sale or promotion, I'm faced with a dilemma.

The logical course of action is to try alternative categories. But with a straight historical novel of a determined literary bent, options are thin on the ground. There's *War*, which usually requires a Sales Rank of #10,000 to #12,000, or maybe 10 copies a day. And, at a stretch, there's *Men's Adventure*, which requires about the same. However, any time I've opted for these categories and was selling enough to appear high on the respective Best Seller lists, that visibility did little to drive sales. Why? Well, I only had to look at the books I was surrounded by in the chart. Readers of Clive Cussler and Tom Clancy are well outside my target market and are unlikely to be attracted to my work.

Unfortunately, this situation occurs a little more frequently than we would like. Our books aren't selling enough to chart in our natural categories, and alternatives are too far removed from our core readership to really move the sales needle. It's especially tough when your natural home is a category with no subcategories (where you can play in the smaller pool while you build your audience). What do you do in this situation?

Luckily, the Best Seller lists aren't the only opportunities for visibility on Amazon. There are the Top Rated lists, Hot New Releases lists, Movers & Shakers, Popularity lists, Also Boughts, and Amazon search results. And we'll cover each of these in turn.

Before you move on, however, I advise you to try to come to grips with the category system. It's not something you're likely to do on a first read, and it will take a little exploring around the Kindle Store (and getting a handle on what sales level is needed to hit certain ranks and certain genre Best Seller lists). I also recommend reading this post *(bit.ly/Visible8)* from historical mystery author M. Louisa Locke to help cement your understanding of the category system (but please note that since that post was written, tags have been removed from the system by Amazon, and you should disregard that section of her post completely).

5. Top Rated

Amazon's Top Rated charts list the Top 100 books in each category and subcategory with the best reviews. The score that determines your placement is calculated using an average of all of the user-submitted reviews for that book on Amazon. You might naturally assume that appearing there is out of your hands, and it is, for the most part. But there are ways you can boost the number of reviews you receive (for better or worse!).

I regularly look at the front and back matter of my books to ensure it is as effective as it can be, and that it is helping me achieve my goals. As I explained in *Let's Get Digital*, I aim to keep front matter to a minimum so that readers who sample the book can get to the meat as quickly as possible. I have single title/copyright page, and then the story begins. Everything else—dedication, author's note, list of other titles, table of contents—gets moved to the back. There is no good reason to have that stuff at the front of an e-book.

The back matter is even more important, but for different reasons. The first thing I want readers to see when they finish my books is a sign-up to my mailing list. Next, I have blurbs for my other titles. Following that, a note requesting reviews. (NB: all of these links should be clickable.) Since I started putting a simple line asking for a review and stressing their importance, my review rate has soared.

I believe reviews are important for a few reasons. A large amount of overwhelmingly positive reviews can help sway a reader who is on the fence; that's inarguable. In addition, most of the big reader sites won't let you advertise unless you have a minimum number of reviews and your average score is above a certain threshold. Finally, if you have enough positive reviews, and your average is high enough, you can qualify for Amazon's Top Rated lists.

While appearing on these Top Rated lists won't drive anything like the same amount of sales as appearing on Best Seller lists, it does provide some impetus. More importantly, though, it gives you a juicy addition for your blurb. *Let's Get Digital* is fortunate enough to appear in three Top Rated lists, and mentioning this in my blurb really helps sway readers (I noticed a difference straight away in the conversion stats from my Amazon affiliate reports).

Finally, if you are in the top three of the Top Rated List for your category, you will appear in the side-bar to the right of the Best Seller list (for those browsing Amazon on computers at least), giving you lucrative front page action. *Let's Get Digital* bounces in and out of the top three for its categories, and that has a noticeable effect on sales.

Appearing on any Top Rated list is a challenge. To give yourself any chance at all, make sure you have a note in the back of your books that requests reviews. And make sure it's clickable. While you won't be able to insert a clickable link when you first upload your book, you should do so at the first opportunity post-release.

I haven't managed this feat for any of my fiction, but several self-publishers have (such as fantasy author Debora Geary). Non-fiction tends to get an easier ride, as you are more likely to be hitting your target market with each sale. As many of you will have experienced, a good run of sales can often be followed by a rash of poor reviews. Authors who crack the Kindle Store Top 100 will be getting a huge amount of new eyeballs on their work, as well as impulse purchasers from outside of their target market, which can often result in negative reviews. A successful free run can have the same result, as can being featured on a big reader site. It comes with the territory, unfortunately, and if you have written a particularly controversial book, the Top Rated lists may be forever out of reach.

Fear not, other lists are much easier to hit. Starting with Hot New Releases.

6. Hot New Releases

The various Hot New Releases lists on Amazon play a key role in determining the initial success of a book. These lists offer crucial extra visibility to newer titles, and appearing on Hot New Releases should be a central part of your launch strategy. It works very similar to Best Sellers—a list of the Top 100 books, ordered by Sales Rank, broken down by category and subcategory. The only books that qualify are those released in the past 30 days, as well as any books in the respective category that are available for pre-order. If you are looking to find the Hot New Releases list, it's placed beside the Top Rated lists, to the right of the Best Seller list for any given category or subcategory (computer browsers only).

Given that pre-order pages aren't available for self-publishers (except a tiny minority who are selling at the very highest level), this is another considerable advantage that traditional publishers have. However, as for Best Seller lists, the lack of attention that publishers pay in choosing the right subcategory (and using all of the categories available to them) is something that can be exploited—assuming you have chosen the right categories for your own work. I can't stress enough how important that is. If you are unclear about this aspect, I urge you to reread *Chapter 4: Categories*.

Hot New Releases should be at the forefront of your mind when planning your next launch. Assuming you have appropriate specific categories (where possible), the next thing you need to do is figure out how many sales it will take to hit the first page of Hot New Releases for each of your categories. If the level of sales required is beyond your book's likely sales performance, then perhaps you need to reconsider those categories again (where possible).

Your aim on release is to hit that front page, and *stay* there. To aid in that goal, you should do two things. First, try to be aware of any big releases in your genre. I was blindsided in Christmas 2011 by the release of twenty backlist titles from Patrick O'Brian, author of the bestselling Aubrey-Maturin historical novels, one of which served as the basis for the movie *Master & Commander*. While my mailing list and social media platform had enough juice to split the pack and put me in the Top 20 Hot New Releases in Historical Fiction momentarily, it didn't have the staying power to keep me there. Quite frankly, there's not much you can do in the face of a wall of books from a giant in your genre. But had I been aware of the rerelease of these books, I would have postponed my launch by a month (the Hot

New Releases list really is that crucial). Given that this was the first time O'Brian's series—one of the all-time top-sellers in historical fiction—had been available on the Kindle, I had no chance. The front page of Hot New Releases was beyond me until my book was no longer eligible for the list.

That was pretty rotten luck, and you are unlikely to face a similar situation, but it can happen. In late 2012, Harlequin mass-uploaded thousands of backlist romance novels from a string of bestselling authors, swamping all of the respective lists. There's not much you can do in a situation like that, other than take the inevitable beating and cut your losses.

There is also something else you need to keep an eye on. As explained earlier, once authors and publishers figured out that Amazon's Sales Rank rewarded velocity, they tried gaming the system by encouraging people to mass-purchase at around the same time. But Amazon's algorithms now push a book back down the charts just as quickly if there is nothing organic behind a one-off sales spike. That might seem counter intuitive, but because of that change, it is now best *not* to tell everyone about your new release simultaneously.

Try to stagger the news of your release over a few days. Even if that means your launch doesn't go as high in the Best Seller list as it could in the first week, it will benefit you in the long run. The algorithms will favor a sustained run of sales—even at a lower level—above a one-off sales spike that goes higher but then dies right away. This might mean hitting your mailing list on the first day, Twitter the next, and pushing the guest post you booked on a popular blog back to the third day. The exact breakdown will depend on your own author platform and mailing list, but the general principle holds: spread the love a little and you have a better chance of hanging on to front-page placement on Hot New Releases, which is your primary goal in your first thirty days post-release.

If your launch goes particularly well, and that front-page action on Hot New Releases leads to further sales and a jump up the Best Seller lists, you might be lucky enough to hit Movers & Shakers, which is covered next.

7. Movers & Shakers

The Movers & Shakers list offers fantastic visibility, but appearing on it is extremely challenging, especially because it isn't broken down into categories. There is only one list, and you must be ranked below #400 in the overall Kindle Store to even qualify for inclusion.

Movers & Shakers is yet another Top 100 list that is ranked in order of sales increase—expressed in percentage terms—over a twenty-four-hour period. If you manage to hit the top three of this list, you will appear on the front page of the Kindle Store Top 100, in between the top three for Hot New Releases and Top Rated, which will get some serious eyeballs on your book cover.

While I have hit the back of the Movers & Shakers list on one occasion, my sales spike was too short-lived to sustain what turned out to be a very brief sortie. And, to be quite frank, most of us will have few opportunities to hit that list. However, it is worth being aware of, as something that can provide extra momentum if you get below #400 in the rankings, despite it likely being out of reach for most authors.

At this point, you might be wondering what your options are. Let's say your book has been out longer than 30 days, disqualifying you for Hot New Releases. A few less-than-glowing reviews mean that the Top Rated lists are unattainable. And the Best Seller lists seem forever out of reach.

How can you get a leg up? How can you get enough visibility to kick sales up to a higher level? The answer is simple: Popularity.

8. *The Importance of Popularity*

The Popularity lists, what they are, and how they are calculated are commonly misunderstood. Readers, writers, and publishers all regularly mistake them for the Best Seller lists, which has led to a lot of the myths surrounding Amazon's ranking system (myths that I covered earlier, including the notion that free downloads count towards Sales Rank). The two lists are quite distinct and have very different algorithms that determine ranking. One thing is similar, though: Popularity lists have a huge influence on the rise and fall of any given book—possibly more influence than anything else on Amazon, and certainly more influence than anything else you can work to your advantage.

Appearing high up on the Popularity lists for your chosen categories is much more achievable than hitting Movers & Shakers, Top Rated, or even the Best Seller lists, and should be a key part of any marketing strategy. But before we get to that, it's essential to understand exactly what the Popularity lists are, where you can find them, and what algorithms feed into them so that you can maximize your opportunities for visibility.

Finding Popularity

The Popularity lists have always been around, but until the very end of 2011, they were largely indistinguishable from the Best Seller lists. They are broken down into the exact same Kindle categories and subcategories, which explains some of the confusion. But unlike Best Seller lists, they don't have a separate listing for free books; both free and paid books commingle. Of course, at the close of 2011, the landscape changed radically with the advent of KDP Select. The corresponding increase in free books on Amazon led to the differences between the Best Seller lists and the Popularity lists becoming much more apparent.

You can find the Popularity lists in three ways. First, they are accessible from the homepage of the Kindle Store *(bit.ly/Visible9)*. The list of categories you see in the left-hand sidebar leads directly to the Popularity lists. Second, if you scroll down to the bottom of your book's product page, you will see the categories you have selected for that title. Clicking on those will also take you to the respective Popularity lists. At this point, you might be wondering what all the fuss is about if the lists are so obscure. But this isn't just about readers who browse the Kindle Store via computers. On all Kindle devices, the Popularity list is what readers are pushed to when browsing the Kindle Store, rather than the Best Seller lists.

Those Kindle browsers number in the millions, meaning that good placement on the Popularity lists can be a *huge* driver of sales. But how are these lists calculated, and how can you improve your ranking?

Calculated Popularity

As I mentioned earlier, the Popularity lists are subdivided into the same categories as the Best Seller lists. But when you first page through them, you will notice a couple of visual differences. There are sixteen books listed per page (six on the smaller-screened basic Kindle), rather than ten per page for the Best Seller lists. Please note though, that Amazon is currently experimenting with a slightly different display—a grid of 24 book covers—so this may be changing soon.

As mentioned in *Chapter 4: Categories*, the number of books in each category is indicated. Unlike the Best Seller lists, which only feature the Top 100 books in each category, the Popularity lists contain *all* the books in that category. While these variances are largely cosmetic, there are more profound differences in the way the lists are determined (please note that the algorithms feeding into Popularity changed dramatically in March 2012, and again in May 2012).

The calculation for Popularity has *nothing* to do with Sales Rank. Rather, your position on the list is determined by a rolling 30-day sales average, *with no extra weight given to the most recent sales*. Also, borrows don't count towards placement, but free downloads do (they're currently worth one-tenth of a sale). And that's not the only bias. One final, crucial, difference with the Popularity lists is that price weighting is in effect, meaning that a sale at $9.99 is worth a lot more than one at 99c.

What is the net result of these differences? For starters, not weighting the most recent sales makes the Popularity lists much more stable than the Best Seller lists. If you can get your book near the top of a Popularity list, it is much "stickier." This is important when developing marketing strategies, which are covered in the following sections, as it means your focus should be on optimal Popularity placement rather than hitting a certain Best Seller list (as the latter should happen anyway if you achieve the former).

Another important conclusion to draw is that while all of this makes the 99c price point less attractive as a permanent price point, it adds impetus to the idea of making your book free for a short spell. Free downloads are only worth one-tenth of a paid sale, but it is a lot easier to give away ten copies of a free book than to convince one reader to open his or her wallet. Indeed, a free run involving several thousand downloads can vault you up the Popularity lists (as those free downloads will be worth several hundred sales in your 30-day average).

You won't see the results straight away, though. One of the quirks of the Popularity list is that it doesn't count the last 40 hours or so of sales, meaning that it could be two days (or more, if the system is laggy, which is often the case) before that free run begins to boost your 30-day average and catapult you up the Popularity lists. It can be another few hours again before you see the results of that increased visibility in your KDP sales reports.

As flagged earlier in the book, while free is still a powerful tool, a successful free run doesn't lead to the crazy sales pattern we saw between December 2011 and March 2012. Understanding why requires a little history lesson. For those not interested in delving deeper into the evolution of the Popularity lists, you can skip this next part. It's not crucial to understanding how the lists work today, but it may help you understand future changes—which are inevitable; Amazon rarely stands still.

The History of Popularity

Amazon occasionally tinkers with the algorithms that feed into the Popularity list, but far less than is popularly imagined (for example, there were only two major changes in 2012). Any future changes may require tweaking your own approach. I regularly describe such changes on my blog *(bit.ly/Visible10)*, so be sure to check in. For the most part, the information I present there (and here) has been tracked and tested by a group of data-crunching authors, two of whom regularly poke and prod the algorithms on their own sites. I recommend following the blogs of Ed Robertson *(bit.ly/Visible11)* and Phoenix Sullivan *(bit.ly/Visible12)* if you want the hard data behind the conclusions I present. They've done all the heavy lifting on this topic, and any kudos should go to them. For the mathematically minded, Phoenix Sullivan has even presented a formula that attempts to capture the base algorithm used to determine ranking on the Popularity lists (see *bit.ly/Visible13* in particular).

I find it interesting to look at how the Popularity list has evolved over the past year. It gives me a sense of where Amazon sees the market going—and Amazon is rarely wrong. Given how tight-lipped Amazon is in general, I find this a fascinating peek behind the curtain. Doing so helps explain why KDP Select gave such stunning results at the start, and how the power of free has been lessened. I'll also attempt to explain *why* Amazon has made these changes, and how there are still opportunities for old-school results in the UK and Europe.

When KDP Select was first launched, the Popularity calculus was quite different. Free downloads were counted as a full sale (as were borrows), and there was no price weighting (i.e. 99c books weren't discriminated against). With this formula, self-publishers who staged a successful free run saw their books shooting up the paid charts two or three days after finishing a free run. Authors who had a number of titles out (and enrolled in Select) saw the best results, as they could make book after book free and the resulting bounce would (often) lift all of their other titles. Some serious money was made until Amazon began making major changes to the Popularity algorithms in March 2012.

Before Amazon arrived at the Popularity list we have today, they experimented with three separate formulas, using split testing to measure the outcome (described in *bit.ly/Visible14* by Ed Robertson). Ultimately, they opted for the current formula (which is pretty much the List B identified by Ed Robertson in the above-mentioned post, combined with some of the price weighting from List C). I should note, however, that this only refers to Amazon US. At the time of writing, all the international Amazon sites are still using the pre-March 2012 algorithms for calculating Popularity lists.

Given that these changes were largely detrimental to self-publishers, some saw this as a harbinger—that Amazon had dangled the KDP Select carrot to tie up more than 100,000 books in exclusivity and had then moved on once these books had served their purpose. However, such an analysis fails to take into account that this last round of algorithm changes was also detrimental to books in Amazon's own imprints (in some ways, at least). For example, the price weighting in the algorithm would seem to disfavor many cheaper-priced Amazon imprint books, and benefit more-expensive traditional best sellers.

As always with Amazon, I think there is a simpler

explanation, one that goes right to the heart of what the company strives to achieve. Amazon's philosophy is simple: recommend the product customers are most likely to purchase. In terms of books, Amazon doesn't care if the title comes from a large publisher, a self-publisher, or one of their own imprints, it will always (attempt to) recommend the book it believes the reader is most likely to want. This philosophy is in stark contrast to the other retailers such as Barnes & Noble, Apple, and Kobo. A cursory glance at their sites will show you that there is a lot more virtual co-op (the online equivalent of those books piled high on tables when you walk into a bookstore) than on Amazon. Getting to the various lists and categories requires customers to navigate past far more "virtual tables." They take a top-down approach to book recommendations, and, of course, they sell those spots to the highest bidder (i.e. large publishers). Amazon's recommendation engine is a lot more egalitarian, and in my opinion, it's one of the key reasons why Amazon is winning.

Amazon's system will recommend a 99c short story published by me over a $9.99 novel published by Random House, if that's what it thinks the reader is more likely to buy—even though it makes them less money. Once you understand that, the algorithm changes make a little more sense, and you can see how they reflect the changing demographics of Kindle owners.

In very simple terms, the first phase was the early adopters, the Boomers, and the heavy readers. These groups were far more likely to be price sensitive. When you read four romance novels a week, the difference between $0.99 and $12.99 *really* starts to matter. But the group of readers switching to e-books now is different. They don't read as frequently. They receive their book recommendations from different places (more from mainstream sources, such as newspaper reviews, and less from things like book blogs). They are the kind of people who would browse what's on the table at the front of the store, rather than delve into the shelves at the back. Their tastes tend to be a little more conservative, a little less adventurous. They feel more comfortable sticking with the names they know. And, as they read considerably fewer books per year, price isn't as dominant a factor in their purchasing decisions.

All of the above is conjecture, of course, but I think it's a plausible explanation as to why Amazon has rejigged the Popularity list, rewarding consistent sellers over those whose sales spike now and then, and rewarding higher-priced books over those that are cheap or free. You may have your own theories; the important thing to note is that not only has the power of free been lessened by Amazon, but it could be argued that they are likely to further dampen it in the future (which I will cover in *Chapter 16: The End of Free?*).

One last thing: critics of Amazon often accuse the company of inspiring a race to the bottom. (Those critics seem to ignore the higher royalties Amazon pays for e-books priced $2.99 and above, and that competing retailers such as Kobo and Barnes & Noble pay higher royalties at 99c, but I digress.) When you examine these algorithm changes, it's clear that Amazon is now encouraging higher prices than it did before. Many self-publishers have followed suit and have managed to maintain sales levels at those higher prices.

I'll delve a little deeper into free and its place in your marketing plans in *Part II: Free Pulsing*, but for present purposes, you should note that free was a tool for Amazon as much as it was for self-publishers. It made owning a Kindle an even more attractive proposition. Not only were there lots of free books for readers to download, but readers also couldn't get many of them anywhere else. But Amazon isn't interested in making all content free. They make a lot of money from the sale of e-books (indeed, Jeff Bezos recently confirmed to the BBC what had already been widely rumored, namely that Kindle devices don't make a profit themselves and the aim is to make money on content purchases). And they also know that the demographics of those who entered the market at Christmas 2012 are very different to those who entered at the tail end of 2010.

Now that free has become a less useful tool for Amazon, we must ensure we have other tools at our disposal as well. It doesn't mean that free is "dead" or that it shouldn't be a part of your toolkit, but authors can no longer depend on it exclusively, as many did in the period directly after the introduction of KDP Select. Instead, we must use a variety of approaches, of which free is but a part. However, before that, we must take a look at the final places on Amazon where visibility can be achieved: Search and Also Boughts.

9. Search & Also Boughts

While the lists described in the preceding chapters provide the main opportunities for your book to gain more visibility, (or, at least, the primary ones that you can influence), not all customers browse via Amazon's lists. Some use the search function on Amazon to find new books to read, so it's important to know how to maximize visibility there.

Amazon Search

For any given search term entered by a reader, Amazon's system will return a list of books that it considers relevant. Relevancy is determined by a number of factors, including keywords (which are chosen when you first upload to KDP), as well as your book's title and subtitle. Tags were only a factor for customers specifically searching via tags, but they were removed altogether at the start of 2013 and you don't need to worry about them at all.

You may not have too much wiggle room with your book's title, although, for non-fiction, putting keywords in the title is *very* important; for example, *Let's Get Digital: How To Self-Publish, And Why You Should* or *Guitar Mastery Simplified: How Anyone Can Quickly Become a Strumming, Chords, and Lead Guitar Ninja.* I'm going to focus here on keywords, which have the most profound influence on whether your book will actually appear under the search term the customer has entered.

You only get to choose seven keywords, so make sure they are relevant to your book. Try to put yourself in the shoes of one of your target readers, and picture the kind of terms they might enter into the search box when looking for books. For example, for my South American historical adventure *A Storm Hits Valparaiso*, I chose *Napoleon, war history, San Martin, historical fiction, Bolivar, literary fiction,* and *adventure,* because my target market is readers of historical and literary fiction, as well as anyone with an interest in South America, Latin America, or the kind of military/sea-faring fiction set in the Napoleonic Era. For *Let's Get Digital,* I chose *publishing, how to publish, publish, self-publishing, how to self-publish, formatting,* and *self-publish.* The inclusion of "publishing" keywords in addition to "self-publishing" ones is down to a trick I learned from author Joanna Penn (whose excellent blog is at *bit.ly/Visible15* and who advises checking the popularity of various terms on Google searches with this tool *bit.ly/Visible16*).

Try searching on Amazon for some of your keywords to see where you appear. You will probably notice that there are several books ahead of yours. The prime real estate (as ever) is anything "above the fold" or viewable without scrolling, which means you really want to be in the top three. But also make sure to check those keywords in the Google tool I mentioned previously. There's not much use in appearing at the top for a term that nobody searches for. While there's no exact mapping between popularity of search terms on Google and Amazon, the Google tool will at least serve as a guide.

Improving Your Search Placement

If you want to appear higher in Search for any given term, you first have to understand how the system determines the ranking. A number of variables feed into the algorithm that determines Search placement, but the most important (and the only one you can really control, aside from choosing good keywords) is Popularity, which was explained in detail in *Chapter 8: The Importance of Popularity*.

The marketing strategies outlined in the rest of this book will have a real focus on maximizing your placement on Popularity lists, and this will have the happy knock-on effect of improving your position in the search results for your targeted terms. A word of warning: you may be tempted to improve your visibility on Search by using a more successful author's book title or name as a keyword (or in the title or subtitle of your book). Aside from the questionable ethics of attempting to cannibalize someone else's hard-won success, you risk Amazon removing your book from sale and suspending your account. Amazon takes such actions seriously, policing this behavior with a heavy hand.

Also Boughts

Once your book has been out for a few days and has registered its first ten or so sales, you will see a string of books underneath your blurb, with the heading "Customers Who Bought This Item Also Bought." Writers tend to get worked up (or excited) about the titles that appear here, but what is much more crucial is where *your* book is appearing. Just because Suzanne Collins is second in your Also Boughts doesn't necessarily mean you are second on hers.

Think about it. If you have sold 500 copies, and 100 of those purchasers also bought the *The Hunger Games*, there's a good chance that Suzanne Collins will be #1 on your Also Boughts. However, she has sold a lot more than 500 copies, and it would take an incredible sales streak to appear at #1 on hers.

With regard to the Also Boughts appearing on *your* book page, the ideal books to appear there are ones that you have written (so readers don't get tempted away to someone else's page). Unfortunately, you have little control over that. The only real way you can influence what appears there is by writing more than one title with the exact same target audience, such as successive books in a series. For example, I expect *Let's Get Visible* to appear at or near the top of the Also Boughts for *Let's Get Digital* (and vice versa), as the target audience is very similar, and I will be tapping into that audience via my blog, Facebook Page, Twitter presence, and mailing list.

To see a more comprehensive example of this, here is the product page for *The Weight of Blood* (*bit.ly/Visible17*), the first book in a popular epic fantasy series by David Dalglish. As you can see, all of the books appearing there are written by him. This has the dual effect of not having other authors advertising their wares on his page and reinforcing the popularity of the series as a whole to potential new readers.

If you are able to tie your Also Boughts together like this, it opens up new marketing possibilities for you with regard to things like cross-promotion. I'll discuss those strategies in more detail later in the book, but here's a quick example so you know what I'm talking about.

After *Let's Get Visible* is launched, it is highly likely that I'll run a 99c sale on *Let's Get Digital* to try to attract new readers to the series. That sale will boost the visibility of *Digital*, but also of *Visible*, because all of those fresh eyeballs will be seeing its cover in pole position in the Also Boughts (assuming everything goes to plan). Conversely, at some point in the future, if the sales of this book take a dip, I'll probably run a similar sale on *Visible*, which will again benefit both books.

You don't need to write in a series to benefit from this strategy, because books written by you in the same genre could easily have prime Also Bought placement on their respective product pages, but it certainly helps. If you are like me, and your output tends to be all over the map (my first four releases were literary fiction, science fiction, non-fiction, and historical fiction!), then it's highly likely that your Also Boughts won't be tied together in this way, which will limit the potential return from any cross-promotion you do across your titles— something to consider when choosing your next project.

Also Boughts don't change as frequently as Sales Rank or Best Seller lists. They generally recrunch twice a week, and you don't tend to see any at all until you get those first ten sales (although you may see a placeholder indicating books Also Viewed by customers until you pass that threshold). Additionally, there's usually a lag of a few days after a new release before that area is populated on your book page (and, crucially, before your new release appears in the Also Boughts of other books), so don't worry if you are bereft of Also Boughts at the start. I should also note that free downloads won't count towards those ten initial sales, but they will still make an appearance in your Also Boughts after you have crossed that threshold—meaning that a free run will change your Also Boughts dramatically (both on your page, and the pages your book appears on), at least for a short time.

10. Battling The Sales Cliff

In the introduction to this book, I described the sales cliff, the point at which your book suddenly turns from a consistent, effortless seller into one wearing concrete boots, plummeting down the rankings. This freefall can be unnerving, but at least it should now be understandable. As outlined in *Chapter 8: The Importance of Popularity*, when you have a sales spike that rolls out of your 30-day average, your book will drop down the Popularity lists. This essentially makes it invisible to the large group of readers who (exclusively) browse the first few pages of your category. If people don't know your book exists, they can't buy it, and a drop in sales is inevitable, followed by a drop in Sales Rank.

The most obvious time a book "cliffs" is about a month after release. All those launch week sales are no longer part of your 30-day average, and your new baby will have a corresponding drop in the Popularity lists. Compounding this, your title will no longer qualify for Hot New Releases—the equivalent of cutting off its oxygen. This double-whammy of lost visibility can have a crippling impact on your numbers.

If you think about it, the situation isn't *that* different to what happens with print books in bricks-and-mortar stores. New releases get a lot of attention, including lucrative spots on the front tables, recommendations by the staff, or extra visibility in a special section in the store. But if they don't sell extremely well in the first month or so, they will be unceremoniously yanked from the shelves and returned to the publisher (or warehoused, and then returned).

There is one key difference with e-books: the virtual shelves are endless. The marginal cost for storing an e-book on Amazon's servers is next to nothing, so they don't particularly care if a given book is not performing. They don't cease stocking it. Because of this, your book doesn't have only one chance to succeed, as it would in physical bookstores. Instead, it has *forever* to find its readers.

What does this mean for you, in practical terms? Your book is never completely dead in the water. It has an infinite amount of "lives." And you can resuscitate its sales through any number of means.

The next three sections of this book will teach how to do just that, taking advantage of your newfound knowledge of the algorithms and Amazon lists to maximize your results. Once again, all of this assumes you have a good book that is professionally presented. No amount of visibility will help a dud, or a book with a crappy cover (or one that doesn't speak to its genre), or a ridiculously high price, or a flaccid blurb, or shoddy formatting, or pages and pages of extraneous front matter that leave little of the actual book for readers to sample. If any of these issues apply to your book, I strongly urge you to read (or reread) *Let's Get Digital.*

For the rest of you, it's time to get visible.

PART II: FREE PULSING

Free Pulsing is a fancy term for setting your book free on a regular basis to boost sales. There are a couple of ways to make your book go free, one via KDP Select, and the other involving setting a book free on a competing retailer, like Apple or Kobo, and getting Amazon to price match. The latter approach is unreliable, convoluted, and not as powerful, but it doesn't require exclusivity and allows for extra options, such as perma-free or price matching by territory. This section will teach you how to make the most of all of these approaches, but will also outline the recent changes Amazon has made to dampen the power of free.

11. Is Free A Bad Idea?

It's quite common to see overwrought blog posts decrying the supposed race to the bottom, complaining that cheap and free titles, and especially self-published titles, are training readers to pay little or nothing for books. The general contention is that slapping 99c on a book devalues its contents, and literature in general, and that authors and publishers who go the extra step and set a book free—even temporarily—are cheapening their work and making it harder for *anyone* to get customers to actually pay for books.

Aside from confusing price and value, what this argument fails to consider is that there has always been plenty of ways to get books for nothing, or next to nothing. Secondhand bookstores have been around forever. Libraries, despite cutbacks, remain popular. Any number of classics are available from publishers at knock-down prices or as free downloads from both retailers and sites such as Project Gutenberg. In fact, you could spend the rest of your life reading for nothing!

Despite this flood of cheap or free literature, there hasn't been any movement calling for Dickens, Shakespeare, or Austen to be removed from the literary canon. Their popularity hasn't waned one iota, and the critics haven't revised their opinions downwards. Being cheap or free hasn't harmed their reputations, nor has it hurt the market in general. In fact, it has made it easy for new generations to fall under their spell.

For authors of a more recent vintage, going free has two huge benefits: discoverability and visibility. Making a title free, whether briefly or permanently, allows readers who otherwise wouldn't have discovered your work to see it, people who will spread word of your books to further readers. But those free downloads also gain you crucial visibility, which leads to the rather more immediate and tangible benefit of increased sales.

Free as a Discovery Tool

Neil Gaiman originally took a strong stance against piracy. However, he noticed that in the countries where he was being pirated the most, such as Russia, sales were increasing, rather than decreasing. With some difficulty, he convinced his publisher to make *American Gods* a free download from their site for a month. Sales of that title through independent bookstores, which was the only data they could get, increased by 300%. Since then, Gaiman has taken to asking audiences how they discovered their favorite author. Gaiman says that very few of the readers he spoke to actually purchased the book new—he estimates it at around 5% to 10%. The rest were lent the book, borrowed it from the library, or were given it as a gift. In other words, the majority of readers discovered their favorite author by getting a book for free, one way or another.

In a digital world, writers can give away their work pretty easily, and it will cost them nothing to do so. Each reader who downloads your book could become a fervent fan who makes a personal mission to spread the word about your book. And on sites like Amazon, authors can give away tens of thousands of copies in the space of a few days.

That's a lot of seeds that may sprout at some undefined point in the future. In the meantime, giving away lots of books on Amazon can make you money *now*.

Free as a Moneymaker

While those seeds are germinating, and while your book languishes in the gargantuan to-be-read pile of the average e-reader owner, going free can have great short-term benefits too.

You should already be aware that lots of free downloads can influence your position on the all-important Popularity lists. Because freebies are currently counted as one-tenth of a sale, thousands of downloads will have a positive impact on your placement, and you will benefit from those numbers until they shuffle out of your 30-day average. (If you are unclear on this, go back and read *Chapter 8: The Importance of Popularity*. It's crucial).

In short, going free on Amazon, if done right, doesn't just *stimulate* word of mouth, it *simulates* it too because the algorithms begin recommending your book to readers on a wide scale.

12. Free Matching

The two biggest e-book retailers, Amazon and Barnes & Noble, don't allow you to directly set a free price through their interface. Amazon does allow authors to price their books free for a maximum of five days out of every 90-day period, but only if authors enroll in KDP Select (covered in the next chapter). That comes at a cost: exclusivity. You may not wish to grant Amazon exclusivity for some or all of your books, and you may be seeking an alternative way to price your books free there. Or you may wish to set a book free for a longer period, even permanently. It is possible—and a similar method can be used to set your books free at Barnes & Noble—but there are a few logistical issues you need to be aware of before choosing that approach.

Price Matching via Smashwords

Before the advent of KDP Select, the most common method of setting a book free on Amazon was via Smashwords. The process is quite simple—on paper. You set a price of $0.00 on the Smashwords Dashboard, wait for that price to filter out to the retailers they distribute to, and then inform Amazon that the book is free on those competing sites.

Having the book free on Smashwords alone will not normally suffice. Amazon's automated price bots that crawl the web seem to ignore Smashwords. The bots only seem to care about Barnes & Noble, Apple, Kobo, Sony, and Google. As such, you will have to wait until Smashwords pushes the free "price" out to the respective partner sites.

Once your book is free on any of the five retailers mentioned above, you can inform Amazon of the free price via a link on your book's product page. I've had the best results from getting two or three friends to do the same, and no more; however, books can, and do, go free on their own, given time. Either way, you must wait patiently to see if Amazon will actually match that free price (which it does at its discretion). Be warned: there's a lot of luck involved. Some books go free right away, others have had to wait months, and indeed, sometimes Amazon won't drop the price to free at all. On average, it seems to take a week or two. Just be aware that the timing of this is very much outside your control, and that you might ultimately be unsuccessful. You might wonder if this contravenes Amazon's terms and conditions, but this is a common misconception. Those rules refer to a prohibition against pricing lower at other retailers, and do not pertain to setting a book free elsewhere. I've had it directly confirmed from Amazon that this price-matching technique is acceptable.

When you want to return your book to the paid listings on Amazon, you first need to set your new price on the Smashwords Dashboard, and then wait for that new price to filter out to all the various retailers where it went free. Some can be quite slow to process that change. You should also be aware that once Amazon matches a price, it will keep it that way until *all* of the other retailers have returned the book to the paid listings. Once it is no longer free anywhere else, you can email KDP and ask them to put the price back up, which they won't do if the book is still free elsewhere. It normally takes a day or two, but it can take longer over the weekend or holidays.

Some authors, myself included, have used free matching via Smashwords to attempt to mimic a KDP Select free run without having to pay the price of exclusivity. We've all had mixed results, to be honest. The problem is that it is all about timing, and any number of things can go wrong. There can be delays in your book going free in the first place, either at the Smashwords partner sites or at Amazon. Even worse, there can be lengthy delays in returning it to paid, both on Amazon itself, and especially at the Smashwords partner sites. Often, one of the retailers (such as Sony or Kobo) can take weeks to put the price back up, leaving your book free on Amazon for that entire period.

If you are attempting to make a book permanently free (which you may wish to do for the lead-in to a series or for a short story in order to promote a longer work), this won't be a concern. But if you are going free to attempt to boost sales you need to be aware that coming back to the paid listings can be fraught with pitfalls.

At the moment, the connection between Smashwords and Apple is lightning fast, so you might consider opting out of the other retailers before attempting this kind of price matching, which will at least reduce the number of things that can go wrong (without obviating them completely, it must be said). The downside, of course, is that your book won't go free on Barnes & Noble, but you will be able to *somewhat* mimic a KDP Select free run without granting exclusivity for 90 days to Amazon. I did this in May 2012 with *Let's Get Digital*, garnering over 25,000 downloads in a five-day period. There was a significant bump in sales afterwards, and I benefited from those numbers with advanced placement on the Popularity List for the following four weeks, which drove further sales.

I must mention, however, that even with everything working quite quickly, I still returned to the paid listings two or three days later than would have been possible had I been in KDP Select. The difference in potential sales was stark. A friend went free over the same period with similar download numbers via KDP Select, but, unlike me, came off free at just the right time. He sold around 250 copies more than me in the following week. So even when everything goes right, the book goes free at the right time, you get mentions from all the big reader sites, *and* you go back to paid as quickly as possible, you still won't be able to fully mimic the effects of a KDP Select run—not via Smashwords at least. But there are other options.

Price Matching via Apple or Kobo

If you upload directly to Apple or Kobo, you will be able to set a free "price." The next step is to get Amazon to price match, and to do so you need to follow the exact same steps as above.

The advantage of going this route is that you have more control over when your book goes free in the first place, which is important if you want to notify sites that your book will be free. (A list of such sites is included in the *Advanced Author Toolkit.*) You also have a *much* greater influence over when your book returns to the paid listings, which is a key factor in how large that post-free bounce will be. The downside is that you won't go free on Barnes & Noble, but you might be able to live with that.

Please note that Amazon sometimes price matches Apple a little more slowly (I suspect their price bots take additional time to notice changes in Apple's black-box system), and that Amazon seems less sensitive to price matching books on Kobo than on either Apple or Barnes & Noble. Indeed, latest reports suggest that price matching to Kobo is very patchy right now.

Price Matching via Draft2Digital

Smashwords has a new competitor in the distribution arena: Draft2Digital. Currently, Draft2Digital can only distribute free books to Apple and Kobo, and it will automatically assign the minimum price (99c) when pushing your free book to Barnes & Noble.

While this won't be of much use to anyone attempting perma-free on all retailers (as the book won't go free on Barnes & Noble), it might be useful for those attempting a short free period. The advantage over price matching via Smashwords is that Draft2Digital allows you to keep your book on sale at Barnes & Noble while attempting to set it free on Amazon. You won't have to worry about Barnes & Noble matching the free price and being sluggish about returning it to paid (and delaying a return to paid on Amazon), as it won't be free there.

Price Matching by Territory

A nice little strategy for boosting sales in hard-to-reach markets outside the US is to price match by territory. If you go direct with either Kobo or Apple, both interfaces allow you to set separate prices in country-specific stores. Once the book goes free in that particular territory, you can then inform Amazon of that price in the usual way, but ensure you do so via the correct Kindle Store. For example, if you want to make a book free on Amazon UK only, set a price of zero on Apple or Kobo for the UK only, and then have a few friends inform Amazon through the link on your book's UK Kindle Store page.

As an added bonus, many of the non-US Kindle Stores (such as all the European sites, including the UK) are using the *old algorithms* for calculating the Popularity list. Free downloads are still weighted as a full paid sale. You can engineer a faux-Select free run in Germany or the UK to light a fire under your sales in those territories, just be aware that all of the above caveats apply regarding Amazon price matching at their discretion, and that there can be delays in returning your book to the paid listings. In fact, it's even less reliable than price matching on Amazon US, but there is also less at risk (assuming the US Kindle Store is your primary market). If, for example, your UK sales are negligible, the worst-case scenario of your book being free for a whole month won't cost you much in lost sales. The potential upside makes price matching by territory a strategy you might want to experiment with.

Perma-Free

You may wish to set a book free permanently, which is a great strategy for the lead book in a series (as long as you have at least two more installments published), or a short story or novella set in the same world as your other books. You can use any of the above methods to set your book free at Amazon, but the only way of setting it free at Barnes & Noble is via Smashwords.

You will have to price match each Kindle Store separately, going free in the US Kindle Store doesn't make your book automatically free in any of the others. Getting books in, say, the German or UK Kindle Store price matched to free is possible, and happens regularly, but can be even less reliable than price matching in the US. In addition, Amazon can simply switch your book back to paid at their discretion, and they do that regularly, forcing you to go through the process of price matching once more. The hassle is worth it, though. This is a proven strategy for driving sales of a series, both on Amazon and elsewhere. In fact, it's one of the few strategies with reliable results for selling outside of Amazon, and has been used by authors such as Sarah Woodbury, David Dalglish, Monique Martin, and Lindsay Buroker. If you write in a series, it's an approach you should strongly consider.

Pricing

When Amazon stops price matching to free, your book will return to the paid listings with the price you had set before it went free. You may be tempted to further boost that post-free visibility by exiting free at 99c. However, if your book is normally priced higher than that (e.g. $4.99) I strongly recommend you don't drop the price until *after* your free run. The reason is simple: while your book is free, Amazon will put a slash through your normal list price and highlight the potential savings to its customers. "Save $4.99" looks a lot more enticing than "Save 99c."

13. KDP Select

Amazon introduced KDP Select at the end of 2011 and it was a game-changer. There are three major components to the program.

1. **Free.** Enrolled titles can be made free for five days of each 90-day period. You can split those days up as you choose, or run them consecutively, but you won't get another set of free days until you begin your next 90-day term.

2. **Borrows.** Amazon Prime customers are able to borrow one title per month from the Kindle Owners' Lending Library, which consists of all Select titles, all Amazon imprint titles, and a small selection of titles from traditional publishers. When an Amazon Prime customer borrows a KDP Select title, the author/publisher receives compensation from a fixed pot, which has averaged around $2 per borrow since the program's inception.

3. **Exclusivity.** Titles enrolled in KDP Select must be exclusive to Amazon for the full 90 days of

each term. This rule only applies to digital versions, and you are free to sell your paperbacks wherever you wish.

The exclusivity requirement caused a lot of consternation, but that was soon eclipsed by the tsunami of success stories. While it was always possible to set a book free on Amazon through "back door" methods (explained in detail in the last chapter), it was never quite understood *why* books tended to have a nice bump in sales post-free if they returned to the paid listings quickly enough before downloads abated.

Because the number of books employing this strategy was such a tiny subset of all books in the Kindle Store, the differences between the Best Seller lists and the Popularity lists weren't obvious. After self-publishers enrolled 100,000 titles in KDP Select in a matter of weeks and began using their free days, the differences between the two lists became apparent. Amazon had given us a powerful tool—perhaps too powerful.

Until mid-March 2012, free downloads were counted as a full paid sale in the Popularity lists. Books with modest returns on their free period, e.g. 1,000 downloads, saw a significant improvement in their Popularity list placement—visibility that immediately translated into sales and a bump up the Best Seller list. Those with a significant return on their free run, e.g. 10,000 downloads or more, usually jumped to the top of the Popularity lists for their chosen categories, resulting in a massive sales spike that often continued for a few weeks.

Everything changed in March 2012, of course, and those changes were made permanent in May of that year. Since then, KDP Select has been much less of a sure thing. Amazon's recent changes to its affiliate program (explained in *Chapter 16: The End of Free?*), along with their continuing experiments in hiding the Top 100 Free Best Sellers list behind a tab, as opposed to side-by-side with the Top 100 Paid Best Seller lists, are simply the latest moves to hamper the power of free.

The relevant question for self-publishers is a simple one. Is it still worth enrolling in KDP Select, given the cost of exclusivity? The answer, unfortunately, is not as simple. You will need to decide for yourself on a book by book basis. But here are some factors to consider.

What Genre Do You Write In?

The big reader sites usually don't feature certain genres (like erotica), and will often warn that one genre or another is probably going to be less successful with their readership. Most use affiliate codes to track clicks and downloads, and they have a very accurate idea of how each book they feature performs.

If the stuff you write is unlikely to be picked up by the major sites (which are usually the only ones that can drive the thousands of downloads necessary to make a dent in the Popularity lists) then you should be realistic about what kind of return you are going to get from KDP Select free runs. Also, keep in mind that certain genres outperform others outside of Amazon (e.g. erotica and romance authors can achieve great success on Barnes & Noble).

Do You Get Borrows?

The other main attraction of KDP Select is the borrow income. Some authors do very well out of borrows, which prove especially profitable on a 99c title when the compensation you receive is around $2, as opposed to the 35c from selling a copy. Some of these authors don't even use their free days; the money they are making from borrows is more than enough to compensate them for any lost income from the other retailers.

Also keep in mind that each borrow counts as a paid sale in terms of Sales Rank calculations. Un-enrolling from the program will cost you any extra Best Seller list visibility you are getting as a result of borrows, along with any visibility you had on the Kindle Owners Lending Library charts. This point is often forgotten, leading some self-publishers to postulate all sorts of nefarious reasons behind a dip in sales after leaving KDP Select. The truth is a little more prosaic: KDP Select gave their books visibility, and leaving took it away.

Can You Sell Outside Amazon?

This book is focused on maximizing your visibility at Amazon for a reason; it's much tougher to gain traction outside of Amazon. I explain why in *Part VI: Selling Outside Of Amazon*, and I outline some potential paths to success in those choppier waters. But I'm not going to sugarcoat it: the odds are against you. If you don't have some kind of plan to reach those readers, you might be better off staying in Select for another 90 days until you do.

Conversely, if you have left KDP Select and the sales on the other retailers are a fraction of what you made from borrows and successful free runs, and your titles are showing little sign of closing the gap through future growth, then you might want to consider returning to the program.

What If Nothing Works?

It is all very well to talk about successful free runs, sizable borrow income, and healthy ex-Amazon sales, but what if none of these apply to you? What if you don't get borrows, your free runs do nothing, and you don't sell outside Amazon? Don't worry, you still have plenty of options.

The next chapter will help you plan for a KDP Select run. If you still get a poor return after following that template, and you aren't seeing any spike in borrows by running your promotions towards the end of the month (so that your books are visible in the Kindle Owners' Lending Library charts when Prime members get a fresh borrow at the start of each month), then perhaps it's time for you to refocus your promotional energies on price pulsing rather than free pulsing, which is covered in *Part III: Price Pulsing*. In any event, Amazon's recent changes (by accident or design) have reduced the power of free, so retooling your approach at this point is probably wise.

14. Planning A Successful Free Run

Like so much in life, the return you get from a KDP Select free run depends on preparation and luck, and the second factor plays a far larger role.

While there are all sorts of sites out there that might feature your freebie, only a handful will direct enough traffic to your book's product page to make the kind of difference you are seeking. To be frank, notifying all of the other sites will either be the icing on the cake of a great return, or the only thing preventing your free run from being a total washout.

Since Amazon started experimenting with new algorithms in March 2012, and made those changes permanent two months later, KDP Select has become much more of a winner-takes-all scenario. With the new calculations, freebies are worth one-tenth of a paid sale on the Popularity Lists. Even if you manage 3,000 downloads, that will only "weigh" the same as 300 sales, or 10 per day for your 30-day average. That will likely result in a bump, but perhaps not a significant one. Fewer downloads than that during your free period will mean a negligible improvement, or none at all.

If your free run gets off to a good start, it's usually best to let it run for all five days at once. But if you don't start off well—garnering fewer than, say, 1,000 downloads on your first day—and you don't have a big site mention lined up for the second day, you should strongly consider pulling the plug and saving your remaining free days for another attempt (note: you can cancel a free run at any point in your KDP dashboard).

Below, I have listed a number of steps you can take to improve your chances of getting a good return from your KDP Select free days, depending on how much time you want to invest. There's also the option of spending a small sum to have your book featured on some sites; however, precious few of those opportunities are worth the money. A more complete overview of how to evaluate any advertising opportunity (whether for a freebie or not) is in *Part IV: Advertising*, but for now I'll simply mention the sites worth shelling out for.

Most sites don't charge at all, but that may change in the future, given Amazon's recent amendments to its affiliate program (explained in *Chapter 16: The End of Free*). As such, the information provided here is correct as of April 2013. I've broken things down depending on how much time you want to invest in this, starting with the steps everyone should take.

Notify Ereader News Today and Pixel of Ink

Neither site currently charges to list a freebie, and each can generate thousands of downloads for every book featured. The competition is fierce, however, and likely to become more so now that Amazon is forcing both to feature fewer free books (explained in the next chapter). To stand any chance of being featured at all, you must have a good review average and a professional package (strong cover, blurb, sample, book).

It certainly doesn't hurt if you have a decent sales record and a track record of performance on their site, either through a previous paid ad or a freebie feature. It helps if the book hasn't been free before, and if it has not been featured by that site before (or at least not recently). Obviously, the bigger authors and bigger genres will always stand a better chance of being featured. That's just the way it is.

Share The Good News

Wherever you are active on social media, such as Twitter, Facebook, Google+ or your blog, make sure you mention the freebie. The return you get from that will depend on the number of followers you have, and more importantly, the quality of those connections. This should go without saying, but don't be spammy. Restrict your posting to where it is allowed (forums often have rules about this), and don't plague your followers with incessant messages. The more desperate you sound, the less enticing the freebie seems.

Create Scarcity

Ensure everyone knows that your book is only free for a limited time; this creates a sense of scarcity—if the reader doesn't act on the deal right now, they might miss it.

Consider Paying For An Ad

If you have the cash, some sites are worth a guaranteed mention. There's an overview of the major reader sites in *Part IV: Advertising*, but suffice to say that a positive return on your investment is far from a sure thing, and only BookBub may fall into that category.

15. Post-Free Tips

Don't spend your time manically refreshing your KDP reports waiting for the post-free sales bump. There will be a delay before all of those free downloads are factored into the Popularity list algorithms and your placement improves. You won't see any significant sales bump (or perhaps any at all), until that occurs.

If your free run garnered less than, say, 5,000 downloads, you may not see any bump at all. Remember that free downloads are only worth one-tenth of a paid sale in the Popularity list calculations, and that Popularity is calculated as a rolling 30-day score. With something like 1,500 downloads, that will only add an extra 5 paid sales per day to your Popularity score, which is unlikely to advance your book on those listings enough to get your book where you want it to be (the first page of your category).

Quite frankly, there's not much you can do with a result like that, except chalk it up to experience, figure out what you can do better next time, and move on.

If your free run was successful, and you got

10,000 downloads or more, you should see a significant improvement in your Popularity placement in the coming days. Don't panic if the bump doesn't materialize after a couple of days. Amazon's system can be very laggy at times, especially when they are rolling out new features. In some cases, however, even an extremely successful free run can lead to no bump. There's not much you can do, unfortunately. I've experienced this myself, giving away 20,000 copies of *A Storm Hits Valparaiso* without any real sales bump at all. It sucks, but luckily such cases are the exception rather than the rule.

Presumably, you won't be so unlucky, and with a successful free run, you will enjoy advantageous placement for the next three weeks. That visibility leads to sales, and those sales improve your Sales Rank and in turn your position on the Best Seller Lists. Enjoy it while it lasts because those free downloads will shuffle out of your Popularity calculations at the end of the 30-day period, and you'll be facing the Sales Cliff once more. A very lucky few books will stick in a good position and hold it for months. Don't depend on this happening to you. Again, it's the exception rather than the rule. Instead, expect your book to slide a month after your free run. Forewarned is forearmed!

At this point, you might be thinking that this whole approach is simply swapping one promotional treadmill for another, and that you need to come up with some ruse every month to keep your book visible.

But that's not quite the case. Yes, you will get optimal results if you plan regular promotions, but you don't need to come up with some wheeze for each title every 30 days. As series writers especially will know, a sales bump on one title usually leads to an increase in the sales of everything else. If you write across several genres (and/or pen names), obviously you will see less of this spillover, but that's to be expected. Readers who enjoy your science fiction novels may not be thriller fans.

It's also okay for sales to dip for a period; sales ebb and flow even for the most successful writers. This is especially true if you are focusing on finishing a book. A new release will give all of your existing work a shot in the arm, as well as give you a new title to play with for promotional purposes. Your focus should always be on producing quality work as quickly as you can. The most successful writers invariably share a common trait: they have lots of books out. However, this focus doesn't preclude promoting existing work. The most successful self-publishers are savvy operators who promote their backlist regularly.

If you have been experimenting with KDP Select for a while, however, you may be noticing diminishing returns from that strategy. The reasons for that are explained in the next chapter.

16. The End of Free?

The establishment of KDP Select led to a surge in popularity of free books. Authors quickly found that setting their books free for a time could lead to a huge bump in sales when the book returned to the paid listings, and readers devoured the increased selection of free books. The landscape of the genre Best Seller lists changed dramatically, with some authors gracing the charts who had never come close before.

Many of these successes were greatly deserved. They were well-written, well-presented books that just hadn't received a stroke of luck or a period of sustained visibility. However, if we're going to be honest about it, given the near-foolproof route to the charts afforded by the old algorithms, some of those hitting the Best Seller lists weren't quite as polished. I suspect that while Amazon intended KDP Select to be a useful tool for gaining visibility, they didn't intend it to be *quite* so powerful. In addition, there's no doubt that Amazon was keenly aware that the then tranche of readers switching to digital were from a demographic that tends to be less adventurous and less price-sensitive, and that they might prefer a chart containing more familiar names.

Whatever the motive, the outcome of the algorithm changes in 2012 was dramatic: an instant reduction in the post-free bounce that self-publishers had come to expect following a free run. Indeed, it became much more of a winner-takes-all scenario, in which a significant number of free downloads (3,000 to 5,000 at the *very* minimum) was needed to stand any chance of a post-free bump, which was even then not guaranteed.

While this was the most obvious move that Amazon made to reduce the power of free in the past twelve months, it's not the only one. Towards the end of 2012, Amazon began experimenting with hiding the Top 100 Free behind a tab. As with the algorithm changes earlier in the year, Amazon was conducting large-scale split testing that was showing the new incarnation (with the Top 100 Free hidden) to certain users based on their browser, device, or location, and showing the old layout—free books alongside the Top 100 Paid—to another segment. As of April 2013, Amazon was still conducting occasional tests that involved hiding the Top 100 Free, and appeared not to have made a decision. I must point out that the motive behind these changes may not have been to target free at all. Amazon is experimenting with a cover-heavy Popularity list display (one particularly suited to tablets and mobile browsers). It's simply not possible to have free books in this new display. But what matters more to me than motive is the result: reduced visibility for free books.

Obviously, if this change is made permanent, it will dramatically reduce the visibility of free books throughout the site, as presently the most downloaded free books aren't just displayed alongside the overall Top 100 Best Sellers in the Kindle Store, but alongside best sellers in every Top 100 category and subcategory too. Although the freebies would only be a click away, the amount of traffic they receive would be greatly reduced. Of course, we can't be sure at this point that Amazon will implement this change. They will analyze the data and make that determination based on what increases sales overall (and how their customers react).

One change Amazon has already made is having repercussions for free books. In February 2013, Amazon changed the terms of its affiliate program to encourage its members to start linking to more paid books and fewer free books. The new rules are rather strict. If an affiliate exceeds certain limits and ratios for free downloads versus purchases, they will receive no affiliate income for that month.

Reader sites were the target of these changes, forcing them to limit the number of free books they were offering. Of course, this means that it is now even trickier to bag a mention from one of the big sites, which self-publishers widely view as a negative development. For writers who were seeing diminishing returns on KDP Select free runs (which is most of them, to be honest), this helped convince them to leave the program and resume distributing to all retailers. That may not be a bad thing, because Apple and Kobo are now finally courting self-publishers, but there's another reason I don't think it is all doom and gloom.

I see self-publishers as the canary in the coal mine. Thousands of us, all around the world, are trying new things all the time and sharing the results. We are mostly one-person operations, so we can make and implement decisions on the fly. As such, we're always a step or two ahead of large publishers. Most trade publishers were just starting to get to grips with the power of free, but we already knew that party was coming to an end. Now, we've moved on to the next thing: breaking down Amazon's algorithms and using that knowledge to position our books for increased visibility and sales. By the time they figure that out, we won't just be on to the next thing, we'll be on to the thing after that. In short, the ever-present fog of war that shrouds the digital battlefield works in our favor. Embrace it!

As for the reader sites, well, they need something to advertise. Given that many of them built an audience on the power of free too, the transition will be difficult for many. But for those that do survive, it's clear that there will be an increased focus on bargain books, and I suspect the 99c price point will become hot again, although this time as a special, limited-time offer, rather than a permanent price tag. In other words, self-publishers will need to transition from Free Pulsing to Price Pulsing, which, as luck would have it, is the subject of the next section.

PART III: PRICE PULSING

Successful authors moved away from the 99c price point in the US as the market became more developed and less dominated by ultra-price-sensitive readers. Many self-publishers found that sales increased even despite them raising their prices. But higher prices allowed them to do something else: run limited-time specials to revive flagging sales. Price pulsing, which is a fancy term for running such a sale regularly, is one of the main ways you can boost your sales. Given Amazon's recent changes which curtailed the power of free, the 99c price point is about to become hot again, and price pulsing will be the strategy *du jour*. This section will teach you how to play with price to maximize visibility and sales.

17. The Benefits of Running A Sale

I laid out my detailed thoughts on pricing in *Let's Get Digital*, but if you haven't read it, or if you need a refresher, you can read the excerpt dealing with pricing on my blog here (*bit.ly/Visible18*). Since that book was first published in July 2011, the US market has become even more tolerant of higher prices. The market has matured and is less dominated by the kind of voracious readers that are extremely price sensitive (when you burn through several books a week, price can be a major factor in your purchasing decisions).

The UK market is a little different and is in the same position the US was roughly eighteen months ago. The charts are still dominated by lower-priced books—from publishers large and small, as well as self-publishers—and pricing cheaply can reap great benefits there. I expect the UK market to begin maturing this year, and that authors can begin edging up prices, but I price lower in the UK for now. While I release full-length works at $4.99 in the US, for the UK market, I drop it to £1.99 (roughly $3).

I haven't simply plucked these prices out of the air. As I stress in *Let's Get Digital*, experimentation is key. Different genres tolerate different prices (for example, historical fiction and non-fiction readers expect to pay a little more than romance readers). You need to find the sweet spot for your own books.

This pricing structure affords me significant room to maneuver when it comes to running limited time sales—usually at 99c—which is very effective for a number of reasons. First of all, it gives you all the benefits of the 99c price point (such as making your book an immediate impulse purchase that doesn't entail much prevarication), with none of the drawbacks (negative connotations from the book being priced so cheaply). Second, it gives the sense of value (everyone likes a deal). Finally, it creates the impression of scarcity (compelling readers to purchase before the price returns to normal).

It must be mentioned that many authors are keen to avoid the 99c price point altogether. It's tough to make real money when you are only earning 35c per copy sold. You have to shift major numbers to make it worthwhile. However, the primary objective of price pulsing is not to make money while your book is on sale (although that can happen), but to make money in the days and weeks after the sale—once you have raised your price again—and your book benefits from greater visibility on the Best Seller and Popularity lists. As you should know by now, visibility means sales.

The mechanics of running such a sale are simple: you drop your price and then you let people know about it through the usual channels: Twitter, Facebook, your blog etc. To amplify results, consider running a group promotion with other authors.

18. With Our Powers Combined

The core logic behind running a group promotion is that the 99c price point *on its own* doesn't function as a discovery tool; in other words, your book won't automatically become visible to readers just because you dropped the price. You have to find a way to get knowledge of that sale out to the wider world, and combining efforts with other authors is a great, cost-effective way of doing that.

I have been in all sorts of group promotions, some with great results, some that barely moved the sales needle, but the factors that influence a promotion's success or failure (outside of luck) seem pretty universal. Here are some of the reasons that a group promotion can do wonders:

1. **Sharing the load**. Organizing a promotion can involve work: contacting reader sites and book bloggers, preparing posts and tweets, and blogging. The more authors you have, the more you can spread the tasks among participants.

2. **Combining powers**. Each author will bring

something different to the table, whether that's a large readership, a big Twitter following, a popular Facebook Page, a reader-filled mailing list, relationships with key book bloggers and reader sites, or a high-traffic blog themselves. Added together, the combined social media platform can be significant and make some real noise when launching the promotion.

3. **Attracting readers**. One author dropping a book to 99c isn't exactly Twitter-bait. Having a good hook for your promo will really help word spread on social media. It could be a group of romance authors clubbing together for Valentine's Day, horror writers for Halloween, or simply a huge group of authors, across all genres, dropping their prices to 99c for the weekend.

4. **Making connections**. Participating in group promotions is a great way to connect with fellow writers, which can lead to all sorts of future opportunities. It can also lead to a cross-pollination of your respective readerships. Bestselling authors like Blake Crouch and Joe Konrath often run promotions together for a reason: they know they are aiming at a similar target market, and that the readers each has managed to scoop up with their own audience-building efforts will likely be interested in the other's work.

Building A Group Promo

I had the opportunity to run my own promotion over St. Patrick's Weekend 2012, involving 32 books from 26 different authors across a wide range of genres. The results were fantastic: the blog post hosting the sale received 7,500 views, generating over 5,000 clicks, leading directly to more than 1,000 sales on Amazon US alone; that was only a fraction of the overall sales the promotion generated, but they were all I could count via the affiliate links on my blog post.

The authors who participated also generated a huge number of additional sales from the visibility achieved when sales launched their books into the charts. They made hundreds more sales again when the books were picked up by a variety of reader sites, large and small. Some authors achieved their best-ever rankings, those with multiple titles out saw spillover sales to their other books, and we all made some nice money. So how do you put together your own promo?

1. **Give the promo a home**. It's not 100% necessary, but I think group promotions like this always work best when there is some kind of "anchor" page that you can point everyone to, like this (*bit.ly/Visible19*). It doesn't have to be a blog post or a webpage, but I think they work best because everything else (Twitter, Facebook, forum posts etc.) can then be used to funnel traffic towards one single location, especially useful if you want to attach affiliate codes to the links.

2. **Use affiliate codes**. The *Advanced Author Toolkit* section at the back of this book will explain how to set up an Amazon affiliate

account. Affiliate codes serve two important purposes. First, they make money, which can be used to defray any costs involved in setting up the promotion. Second, they provide you with data. When I ran my promo, I was able to provide data to participating authors halfway through the promotion. Some were seeing lower conversion rates than others (i.e. a lot of people were clicking on their links but not purchasing), but when they put a stronger call-to-action in their blurbs, conversion rates rose significantly.

3. **Drive traffic**. You will need all participating authors to pull their weight and tout the promo on their respective social media platforms. Rather than each author blogging about it separately, I think it's best if you get them to direct their contacts to the homepage of the promotion. Some authors may have less time to pitch in than others, and anything you can do in advance, in terms of preparing tweets or Facebook posts, will help make sure everyone hits their networks.

4. **Contact reader sites**. Book bloggers and review sites usually love hearing about these promotions, as it gives them an opportunity to present a bargain to their readers. Again, you will get better results if you prepare everything bloggers or reviewers need in

advance. If there's a graphic designer among the participating authors, producing a banner or graphic for the promotion really helps make it look professional and enticing.

5. **Run a competition**. An exciting competition will help drive traffic to the promo page and acts as an extra hook for reader interest. Participating authors can split the cost of the prize, and affiliate income can help there too.

6. **Drop the price in advance**. System glitches can often result in a price change not taking effect when you want it to. There's nothing worse than having to pull a book out of a promotion, or having to tell a bunch of reader sites that one of the books they are advertising as a bargain deal has to be removed. Ensure all participating authors drop their price well in advance, but also tell them not to let anyone know about the sale until it's officially due to start—you want to concentrate sales over the intended period in order to rise as high as possible up the charts.

The main objective with any group promotion should be to sell as many books as you can, of course, but also to increase your placement in the Best Seller list for your chosen categories when the promotion ends and your book reverts to full price (yet another reason choosing the right category is crucial).

If your sales are still trending upwards when the

promotion formally ends, it might be a good idea to keep that discounted price going until the wave fades. More likely, things will have already begun to tail off before the promotion comes to a halt. Judging when to raise a book's price is always tricky and you will have to play it by ear. I usually set myself a certain Sales Rank threshold, and if the book dips below that, I raise the price back to normal. Other times, I raise it immediately to maximize income from that visibility. Have a look at the other books around you in the chart. If your book is the only one at 99c, you should raise your price without question. This might sound like a bit of a guessing game, but you will get a feel for it over time.

When your price is back to normal, you should see an uptick in sales arising from the superior placement both on the Best Seller lists and the Popularity lists (as well as Hot New Releases if your book is new). If the promotion went spectacularly well, you might have also received a boost from appearing on Movers & Shakers (as well as bragging rights). However, it's rare for a group promotion to have enough juice to achieve that on its own. For that kind of power, you need some advertising.

PART IV: ADVERTISING

Advertising often gets a bad rap and is seen in some quarters as a waste of money. Part of the reason is that there are so many advertising "opportunities" out there, and some of them are worthless. But the blame for that doesn't just fall at the feet of website owners making promises beyond what they can deliver. Writers also often *knowingly* shell out for expensive ads when they are fully aware they won't receive a positive return on investment, telling themselves it will have an intangible benefit somewhere down the line; quite frankly, that's a waste of money. You will learn which sites are actually worth advertising on, which are worth notifying about free books, and also how to tell if someone is over-egging the kind of results you can achieve with them. Finally, I'll explain how to maximize the visibility any ad will give you, and how to make the most of residual sales in the crucial days *after* the ad.

19. Why Advertise At All?

Some authors are dead-set against advertising. They may have tried running an ad and received miserable results, or they simply insist that the only thing that sells books is word-of-mouth and that advertising is nothing but a waste of money. There is some truth there, but let's look at what word-of-mouth actually entails. If you break it down, it is simply recommendations being passed from one person to another. Those recommendations only carry weight if you trust the source. I have friends who have similar tastes to mine, as well as other friends who like very different books.

But we don't just get recommendations from people. Newspapers, websites, and blogs can all act as a trusted source of recommendations for readers. In fact, a whole "recommendation eco-structure" has sprung up around e-readers, and in particular the Kindle, which recommends books to hundreds of thousands of readers every day. Being featured on reader sites can result in anything from a barely noticeable bump in sales to a spectacular run at the top of the charts.

Featured spots on a multitude of reader blogs and websites are available for writers to advertise their books. The sites all have their own rules and restrictions about what they will feature, as they know that if they don't continue to recommend quality books, their audience will go elsewhere (because they will no longer function as a trusted source).

Advertising on the most popular sites can bring you tremendous results, particularly when combined with a free-pulsing or price-pulsing approach. In other words, if you add the power of a big reader site to a free run or a 99c sale, your book can zoom up the charts.

As the potential for author profit is so great, there are plenty of sites that make promises they can't keep. Some are a little disingenuous about the size of their audience or the level of their readers' engagement, so it is important to have a way to determine what sites are worth your money and what sites should be avoided.

20. The Major Sites

One of the reasons it is so difficult to gain traction outside of Amazon is that it's really hard to engineer the kind of sales spike needed to crack the Best Seller lists on the other retailers. Viable advertising opportunities (i.e. those with a positive return on investment) are thin on the ground. This is partly because of Amazon's dominance—someone investing in a reader site is naturally going to gravitate toward the most popular device, and catering for different device owners is tricky for a number of reasons—but there is another factor that might be even more influential.

Amazon's popular affiliate program can be extremely lucrative for site owners. The most successful reader sites make *serious* money through affiliate sales, far outstripping anything they make by selling ads to writers and publishers. Their book links have affiliate codes embedded in them, which earns them a percentage of the sale of those books and anything else that particular customer purchases on Amazon. (I explain how to set-up your own affiliate account in the

Advanced Author Toolkit section at the back of this book. I strongly urge you to do it, both to make extra money and to collect crucial data for your marketing efforts.)

Barnes & Noble stopped paying out affiliate money on the sale of e-books in early 2012 (an incredibly dumb move). While Apple and Kobo have affiliate programs, neither of those are as well-publicized or as lucrative as Amazon's. As those of you with Amazon affiliate accounts will know, real money can be made when the customers you send to Amazon don't just purchase books, but groceries, laptops, golf shoes and the million other items Amazon sells. All of this greatly reduces the appeal of building a reader site for anyone other than Kindle owners; thus, we are left with the current situation, in which the best advertising opportunities tend to be on sites solely targeting Kindle owners.

The Big Dogs

The top three reader sites are, unquestionably, Ereader News Today, Pixel of Ink, and BookBub. Advertising places on all three sites are highly sought after because of the sites' stellar track record in shifting books. All three have a variety of advertising options, and all have different restrictions on what they will and won't advertise. The first move you should make is to subscribe to their respective newsletters to check out their listings.

1. **Ereader News Today**. Two primary

advertising options with ENT are worth looking at. The first is the Book of the Day sponsorship, which receives prime billing on their daily newsletter, their website, and their Facebook Page. ENT opens bookings for this sponsorship only once a year, and spots are usually filled immediately. If you get an opportunity to grab one of these sponsorships, do so without hesitation. The price is $50 to advertise a 99c deal or $100 to advertise a $2.99 deal. My own experience and the results I've seen indicate that advertising at 99c is a far better option (except perhaps for a box set). As demand far outstrips supply, ENT usually puts up a special order page for a couple of days, and then takes it down again, but keep an eye on the site and on places like KBoards for the announcement around the new year. The second option at ENT worth considering is the Bargain Books advertisement. While this doesn't get the same prime billing, it is effective at selling books, and the price can't be beaten. ENT will only charge a fee of 25% of whatever sales you make via their affiliate code. You literally can't lose money on this ad. They normally take bookings for this ad spot a month in advance.

2. **Pixel of Ink**. This reader site has recently changed up its advertising options. They had been closed to ads for some time, but I find it is

always worth keeping an eye on the site to see how changes develop and to subscribe to their Author Newsletter (*bit.ly/Visible20*) to receive updates. POI had a similar Book of the Day sponsorship to ENT (with similarly spectacular results), but they are now focusing more on multiple 99c deals each day. The good news for authors who used to struggle to get a spot on POI is that there are more opportunities to get featured, and it doesn't cost a thing. The downside is that you don't get a guaranteed placement and you can't pick which day you will run even if you do get chosen. You can submit the dates of your sale here (*bit.ly/Visible21*).

3. **BookBub.** The newest of the three big reader sites has the most juice, but it also has prices to match. BookBub operates on a very different model to the two sites mentioned above. Instead of one large mailing list that recommends bargain book deals in all genres, BookBub has segmented its lists by genre, and has been amazingly successful at building lists that can really shift books. It prices differently too: a sliding scale that varies with the advertised book price and the book's genre. Depending on what you are advertising, and how much you are charging for it, you can pay anything from $40 to advertise a free giveaway to the YA list, or a staggering $1,200 to advertise a $2.99 deal to

Bookbub's Thriller list of 480,000 subscribers (full price list here *bit.ly/Visible22*). BookBub only features books that are either free or are discounted by at least 50%. As most self-publishers price at $4.99 or below, most will only have the option of advertising a 99c deal. These are significantly cheaper ($480 for the Thriller list or $180 for Fantasy), but still represent a significant cost for the average writer. While results are often stunning, and authors can make a great deal more than they handed over to BookBub, not everyone breaks even. You should pay particular attention to previous results in your genre before you advertise. Many titles get turned down for BookBub ads, too. You need to ensure you have a great cover and sufficient reviews. BookBub seems particularly keen on reviews from book bloggers and traditional sources, so make sure you have pulled out any juicy quotes from such sources in your Amazon blurb, or added editorial reviews to your book description on Author Central. If you get turned down, try again when you have more reviews.

The Chasing Pack

Things change extremely fast among the small-to-medium sites, a process accelerated by Amazon's recent affiliate changes. The best way to keep on top of the changes is to monitor the respective threads in Kboards (*bit.ly/Visible23*) that regularly pop up tracking advertising performance on the various reader sites. Here's a couple I'd like to quickly highlight.

Free Kindle Books and Tips (*bit.ly/Visible24*) is currently transitioning to Kindle Books and Tips, a site, as the name might suggest, that will focus more on bargain reads than curating the free listings. The initial results have been very positive from an author perspective, and the site now offers a couple of different advertising options.

BookBlast (*bit.ly/Visible25*) is a site managed by the people behind Kindle Fire Department, which is taking the BookBub approach of segmented email lists. While the subscriber list is considerably smaller, the prices are too. As they seem to be growing nicely, BookBlast is one to watch.

These are only some of a plethora of sites out there competing for your advertising dollars. Many are promising venues with big potential, but many more make grandiose claims with little to back it up, other than the price tag. And things change so fast in this arena that a small site today could be a real contender tomorrow, or they could start charging too much money. The next chapter will teach you how to evaluate *any* advertising opportunity.

21. How to Evaluate an Advertising Opportunity

New sites spring up all the time. Some are worth experimenting with (as long as their prices aren't too high), but others are best avoided. How do you evaluate whether an advertising opportunity is worth the cost? Well, there are a number of metrics you should look at:

1. **Traffic.** Most sites will have information on their advertising page about how much traffic they get. If they don't, ask them. They should be able to provide this information to potential advertisers, and not doing so is a major red flag. Obviously, the bigger the better, but be careful. I've seen plenty of sites claim to have far more traffic than can be verified. One way of checking is to look at the Alexa ranking of the site (*bit.ly/Visible26*). The number you should be particularly interested in is the score for the US (rather than the raw score), as that's where most of your readers will likely be and where the highest penetration of e-reader ownership is.

2. **Mailing list.** Rather than sit and wait for readers to come to them each day, most sites will mail out the various deals to their subscribers. If the site doesn't quote their mailing list numbers, ask them.

3. **Facebook.** These days, a key component in a successful reader site is a thriving Facebook Page. It's very important not to get seduced by the raw number of Likes they have on their page. Facebook made changes to how updates are displayed to users in mid-2012. If a follower doesn't engage with that Page in any way (i.e. Like their updates, click on their links, comment, or share) then Facebook starts to hide updates from those Pages. As such, what you are looking for is a Page with high engagement levels: lots of Likes, clicks, comments, and shares on the posts themselves (rather than the Page). Only then can you be confident that a good chunk of the readers liking the Page will actually see the books promoted there.

4. **Results.** Some sites have a section detailing the results people achieved advertising there, but be aware that they may be cherry-picking data or presenting out-of-date information (some sites used to be very effective, but no longer are). The *best* thing to do is to track a few books yourself, particularly those in your genre. Make a note of

the ranking prior to the promotion (or when it is first posted), and then look at it again later on, and then again the following day. Using the *Rank to Sales Estimator*, you should be able to get a rough idea of how many copies the author shifted.

Consider *all* of the above before parting with your money (unless it is a proven site that you know still gets good results like Ereader News Today, Pixel of Ink, or BookBub). Pay particular attention to how books in your genre do. There's no point spending money promoting your fantasy novel when the site under consideration only gets good results with romance or thrillers.

When evaluating your own performance, don't get *too* excited about rank alone. It's really about sales, and, indeed, the money you make not just on the day in question but in the week after the feature. While appearing on a genre Best Seller list is great for bragging rights, it is more important to consider how many copies you shift on the day, and *crucially*, how many you sell once you raise your price back up to capitalize on that visibility.

Pricing

Most sites require that you drop the price of your book to 99c (or sometimes $2.99) for the duration of the promo, which is normally just for one day. Obviously, it's hard to make money at 99c. You need to shift a hell of a lot of units to be successful when you are only earning 35c per sale.

A common approach is to let the 99c (or $2.99) price ride until the book peaks, and then jack it up to your normal price as soon as the book starts to slip. This is where the real money is made. When you are earning more than $2 per sale (if your book's normal price is $2.99), or around $3.50 per sale (if the normal price is $4.99), it quickly adds up. You may want to hold on at the lower price point if you are getting good visibility on a Best Seller list. Set yourself a certain point in the rankings (e.g. #1000), and if you slip below that, raise your price.

This is something you will need to judge on a case-by-case basis and experiment with. Of course, if your book is still climbing the rankings, you should probably leave it as is. Raising the price will likely reverse that trend, and it's almost always best to wait until slippage begins before you raise your price.

22. Evaluating Your Promo

Whether your promotion can be considered a success or not will depend on what you were attempting to achieve. This book encourages authors to look at promotions through a strict prism of return on investment, because that is the surest way to avoid being out of pocket; however, that doesn't mean that you only evaluate the performance of the ad based on that day's sales. If you have done things right, there should be residual sales in the week *after* the ad.

I suggest measuring both the sales on the day itself (factoring in the reduced royalties), and then looking at how much extra you sold during the following week when compared to the week before the ad. Series writers, in particular, should also monitor collateral sales. Promoting the first book in a series will usually lift the second, but all sales that are above your weekly average on any of your titles should be counted when evaluating the promotion. I think it's best to look at it in dollar terms rather than units sold, and then compare that to the cost of the ad. (A similar approach is useful when judging the effectiveness of a free run via KDP Select.)

Categories Redux

Before you run *any* promotion, make sure your book is in the right categories for your expected level of sales. You can get a rough estimate of the sales you can expect from looking at the performance of other books in your genre. While you may have chosen smaller, less-competitive categories in the past to reflect your sales level, remember that a good promotion will allow you to compete at a higher level. Ideally, you want to maximize your visibility.

Also, switching categories can be a good idea if you have recently tapped out some of your former audience with a successful free run. New categories will mean fresh eyes on your book, and a category change can help give sales new momentum.

Back to Popularity

After the sales spike subsides, you might think it prudent to switch back to the smaller categories that you normally compete in, but stay your hand for now. A couple of days after the beginning of your sales surge, you should start jumping up the Popularity list as the promo sales are factored into your 30-day average. This extra visibility can further spur sales, and your book could rise even more (or, at the very least, those additional sales might help slow your book's descent).

At the same time, however, you will be battling a new wave of books that may have sales spikes of their own, or that may be coming off a successful free run. They may jump above your book, pushing yours further down. You will need to watch your placement on the respective Popularity lists and decide for yourself when a category change is wise, depending on how your title is doing.

If you are getting pushed down past the first few pages of the Popularity list for your chosen categories (and especially if you are no longer appearing on the Best Seller list and have no upcoming promotion to boost your 30-day average) then you might consider a change. If freshening up your categories will do nothing for you, or if there are no suitable subcategory alternatives for you to choose from, you might have to accept the slide with grace. There's nothing you can do about that until your next opportunity for promotion.

Of course, it is easier to boost the sales of a book that is already doing well. In the next section, you will piece together all the knowledge learned so far to ensure that your next release gets off to the best possible start, right from launch day.

23. Combining Promos

If you've had the pleasure of an ad-supported raid on the charts, you will likely have also experienced a similarly rapid plummet back into the primordial ranking ooze. It's somewhat inevitable, given that your book was visible to tens of thousands of new readers all of a sudden and then, just as suddenly, wasn't. However, there are ways to prolong your run at the top, and it all comes back once again to Sales Rank.

At the start of this book, I explained that to prevent anyone gaming the system by organizing a group purchase of a book at the same time, Amazon's system recognizes a one-off sales spike and pushes such books down the rankings just as quickly as they rose. You have several tools at your disposal to combat this.

The most basic way is via category selection, which I recapped in the last chapter. Visibility in any given category alone usually isn't enough, on its own, to be self-sustaining, but listing your title in the right categories can at least slow your book's decline after the initial burst from your ad feature has subsided. Running promotions in concert with each other can help sustain your book's sales level a little longer. You might think running consecutive promotions is simply postponing the inevitable, and it is to an extent, but the post-promo period—after your book has reverted to full price or to a paid listing (after being free)—is where you make the real money. The longer you can stretch out that period, the more profitable it will be. Indeed, the longer you can keep that sales run going, the greater the chance is that Amazon will start recommending your book on a much wider scale using its own internal promotion, such as email blasts.

PART V: LAUNCH STRATEGY

In this section, we will take all of the knowledge you have learned about the lists that give your book crucial visibility, and the many ways in which you can gain position on those lists, and apply it to a new release. I'll describe a typical book launch and explain how doing one of those can actually hamstring your chances. But don't worry, I'll provide alternatives. The first is a pretty dependable way to launch any book. The next pair are high-risk strategies that will only suit certain titles but can culminate in stellar rewards. Whatever you decide, one thing will influence your success enormously: a healthy mailing list.

24. Building A Mailing List

What happens when a reader finishes your e-books? What's the first thing they see? What's the first thing they do? Back matter is extremely important, a golden opportunity to solidify the connection that your story has created with your readers.

The basic components of effective back matter are fairly straightforward: blurbs for and/or links to your other books, links to whatever social media presence you have, a short note requesting reviews, and, most important of all, a link to your New Release Mailing List (mine looks like this *bit.ly/Visible27*).

If you don't have a mailing list already, you need to set one up immediately as it's one of the most powerful tools at your disposal. Without an effective method for collecting readers' emails (which I'll get to), every time you have a sales spike, every time you go on a free run, you are missing out on a huge opportunity to build a sustainable future for yourself as a writer.

Authors and publishers regularly gripe about Amazon. They fear depending on a third party. They worry about diversification and independence. But many of them don't do the single most important thing to build that independence and ensure that their future financial health is not at the mercy of someone else.

Without a mailing list, most of your readers will still find your other books. Amazon's system does a pretty good job of recommending books by the same author, and they aren't too hard to find if a reader noses around a little anyway. Outside of Amazon, it's a little more challenging—given the deficiencies of its competitors—but not impossible.

But even if the various retailers' systems for recommending other titles by the same author were perfect, having a mailing list would still be crucial. You don't want to wait until Amazon's system eventually gets around to recommending the next book in the series to your readers; you want to concentrate those sales during launch week to win your book crucial visibility right from the start.

In the traditional publishing world, when a major author like Dan Brown or Stephen King has a new release, it's accompanied by a huge marketing budget and you will see ads all over the place: newspapers, billboards, and public transport.

The main aim of this advertising is not to bring new readers to these authors, but to announce to existing readers that the book is out. The hope is that enough fans will hear about the new release and buy it during launch week, thus pushing it high in the print

Best Seller lists, giving the book lucrative visibility from which it will likely kick on and sell a ton more.

The strategy for self-publishers and e-books is somewhat similar, but it doesn't require the same kind of marketing spend, or indeed any. If you have been diligently collecting readers' email addresses from the beginning, you will already know the power of your mailing list. Hitting that list when you release a new book can really launch it up the charts, first gaining you traction on the various Hot New Releases lists for your chosen categories, and then hopefully pushing you onto the respective Best Seller lists.

Without such a mailing list, you are merely hoping that your existing readers hear about your new book, and that they buy it relatively quickly. There really is no logic in ignoring such a powerful tool, but it's never too late. If you don't have a mailing list, start collecting names *today*.

To avoid confusion, I'm not referring to your blog mailing list, but a specific list of names of readers who want to be notified about new releases. I'm also not referring to the new Amazon feature (launched April 2013) which automatically notifies readers when authors of their choice release something. Aside from the fact the latter isn't working terribly well at the moment, that's *Amazon's* list, and they won't share. You need your own. A list you control.

Mailing List Providers

I use MailChimp. It's free (within certain limits), it's powerful, it has a good record of avoiding spam filters (which is crucial), it has great tracking (so you can see who clicked what, and tweak successive emails accordingly), and it produces very pretty emails without any graphic design skills needed. The interface can be a little fiddly, but with a bit of tinkering you can get pretty looking emails like this (*bit.ly/Visible28*).

One of the only drawbacks with MailChimp is that it's only free up to 2,000 subscribers. But if you have that many on your list, money is probably not as pressing a concern as it used to be and you can either spring for MailChimp's paid service, or an alternative provider like AWeber or SMTP–which many consider better value once your list starts really growing.

Capturing Email Addresses

Once you have set up MailChimp (or your preferred provider), you will be given a link to your mailing list sign-up page. The default form is fairly basic and boring, but you can customize it by following these instructions (*bit.ly/Visible29*).

You can place this link anywhere you like: your blog, your Facebook Page (via a nifty app), and, most importantly, in the back matter of your books. The latter is the most crucial of all. I strongly urge you to put a *clickable* link to your mailing list at the back of all your books; it should be one of the first things readers see when they finish your story. Of course, this doesn't just hold true for new releases. You should add this clickable link to all of your books right away.

Don't be tempted to add anyone to your list without permission. Aside from being against the law, when your mailing list grows to a decent size, you will be in the stupid position of paying to send emails to people who have no interest in receiving them. Be aware of all applicable laws regarding spam, such as CAN-SPAM legislation (*bit.ly/Visible30*). Your mailing list provider should have resources to help you remain in compliance.

The Right Tool For The Job

Some people use their mailing lists to send out a newsletter that is filled with all sorts of odds and ends, but I'm not sure that's the best approach (for me, at least). If people want to know what I'm up to, I have a blog, a Facebook Page, and a Twitter account. They can choose their preferred method of social engagement.

If you don't have a blog, you could try the newsletter approach, but bear in mind that some people will be concerned you will clutter their already overflowing inboxes with unwanted crap. As such, I exclusively use my mailing list for announcing new releases. I put in a simple line or two, which varies depending on the book but usually says something like, "To hear about new books first, sign up to my New

Release Mailing List." You can tweak that message depending on the book in which it appears. "Want to find out what happens to Laura? Her next adventure will be released in October. Sign up to my mailing list to be the first to know it's out." You get the idea.

Try to drive sign-ups every so often. Some writers do that by offering discounts, or by giving those who sign up a free short story, but many (myself included) believe that attracts free-hunters who have little interest in buying anything. One way I try to entice readers to sign up is by assuring them that mailing list subscribers will hear about new releases before anyone else. If you post excerpts of your upcoming releases on your blog, or do things like cover reveals to drum up interest prior to a release, that's the perfect time to point people towards your mailing list (like I did here *bit.ly/Visible31*).

That post got me 50 new mailing list subscribers straight away, people who are reasonably likely to purchase my next book immediately on release, pushing it up the charts and gaining it crucial visibility; as you should know by now, that can have a multiplying effect on your sales with no further effort on your part.

The real test of your list, however, comes when you launch a book.

25. The Standard Book Launch

Conventional wisdom recommends a simple way of launching a book. Namely, as soon as your book goes live on Amazon, you tell as many people as possible, hoping that most of them purchase it as soon as possible.

You hit your mailing list, your blog, Twitter, Facebook—all one after the other. You make as much noise as you can, and you excitedly watch the book climb the rankings. At the end of the day, you congratulate yourself for cracking the Top 1000 on Amazon, hitting a few genre Best Seller lists, and selling 120 copies. A great first day, right?

But then the book starts to slide. It's inevitable, you tell yourself. Can't be avoided. It's the new release glow that's fading. Publicity is waning. All those tweets and retweets have slowed to a trickle. But it's okay, you say, partly in hope. Once the reviews come in, things will pick up. Once those first purchasers get through it, they'll start spreading the word and sales will rise again. But they don't. They just trundle along at a gradually decaying level, never recovering. Then, a month after release, things really collapse, and you reach for your wallet looking for some site—any site—to advertise a sale.

It's a pretty familiar pattern, and at this point, I hope you are beginning to understand why. Those launch week sales put you high on the Popularity lists because your 30-day average only included those first seven days of sales, which were really strong. But as new days got added, that average score weakened, and it continued to weaken with each day of lower sales; that led to a drop down the Popularity list each time it recrunched, which in turn lowered your visibility, which meant fewer people were seeing your cover, fewer people were clicking on your book, and fewer people were buying it. It became a vicious circle that had a knock-on effect on your ranking, and on your position on Best Seller lists. Then, a month after release, those launch week sales fell out of your Popularity list calculations altogether, and your book suffered a big drop. On top of that, you no longer qualified for Hot New Releases, so visibility was curtailed further.

Perhaps at this point you scheduled an ad, or set up a group promotion, or dropped the price to 99c. Maybe you scheduled a free run and hoped for the best. Even if that was successful, and the rank rose for a while, you would have faced the exact same situation a month later. Pretty soon, a few months down the line, you're left with a busted flush. There's nowhere left to go. You've tapped out the major sites. You have no more free days left. And your next book isn't out for another three months.

I've faced this situation myself. Like many of you, I've watched with a mixture of envy and admiration as other authors launched their book and managed to make it stick at the top of the charts. How do those authors do it? Is it just blind luck? Well, in some cases, yes, it's nothing more than luck. In fact, you could make the argument that any book that breaks out like that is a matter of dumb luck. But what if there are ways to narrow the odds? What if there is another way to launch a book? A way that gives you consistent sales over that opening month, instead of a spike followed by a slow, horrible decay?

One common mistake writers make when launching a book is rushing to tell everyone immediately. I understand that temptation. You have a new baby and you *need* to tell the world about it! But you should wait. When your book goes live on Amazon, you should first purchase a copy yourself. This is important for two reasons. First, you need to page through it and check that the formatting is correct (this is also a good time to insert a *clickable* link in your back matter asking readers to consider leaving a review). Secondly, and *much* more importantly, you should wait until that first sale registers and you have a rank.

While sales normally appear in your KDP interface one to three hours after the purchase is made (that's when the system is behaving normally; glitches can drag that out for *hours* longer), new releases can take twelve hours or more to gain a rank. You won't get your first ranking until at least an hour after your first sale registers, sometimes longer. Sales that take place before you have a rank won't influence that rank as much. If you tell everyone about your new release the second it goes live, you will miss out on crucial visibility as the book climbs the rankings and hits various Best Seller and Hot New Releases lists.

That's the easy part, and it is something everyone should be able to do without difficulty. But it is only one tiny aspect of putting together a successful, *sustainable* launch. The rest of what I'm about to tell you is a little more counterintuitive, but bear with me. In this section, you'll learn three alternative launch strategies, all designed to combat the death spiral I described earlier. The first should be manageable for everyone. The following two are a little harder to pull off, and a little riskier. But you'll have options, all of which are superior to the standard launch approach you've probably been using so far. The first, I call *Spreading the Love*.

26. Spreading The Love

How do we avoid what seems to be an inevitable downward spiral after the first few days of a book launch? How do we get a little love from the algorithms so that Amazon does the selling for us? As I warned earlier in this book, this strategy is a little counterintuitive, but bear with me. It will require a little discipline from you, because you must resist the temptation to scream your news from the rooftops. I'm suggesting something a little different: a drip feed.

The logic is simple. As soon as authors and publishers figured out that the algorithms that decide Sales Rank placed the greatest weight on the most recent sales, they attempted to coerce as many people as possible into buying at an appointed time, knowing that would cause the chosen book to rocket up the rankings. That still works, because countering that strategy directly would require removing that heavy weighting of recent sales, but Amazon dealt with it in another way: tweaking the algorithms to push a book down just as quickly. Amazon's new system will recognize a one-off sales spike, and the book will fall just as fast afterwards.

How can this be avoided? Well, by ensuring it isn't a one-off spike. Instead of simultaneously announcing your new release on Facebook, Twitter, your blog, and to your mailing list, you should spread the love a little. For instance, hit your mailing list on the first day. Flood Facebook and Twitter the next, and then your blog on day three. Save that juicy guest post or interview for the fourth day. Depending on your own social media mix, you may need to tweak the formula. For example, if you are huge on Facebook and have an active page that drives a lot of sales for you, it might be worth splitting that out into its own day. And if your blog has a small audience, or you aren't that active on Twitter, you may need to roll those two together (possibly even with something else, such as a guest post).

This approach won't move your book as high up the rankings as hitting everything all at once will, but don't worry, that's part of the plan. The aim is to show the algorithms that this isn't a one-off sales spike: that your title is able to sustain sales. Three or four days of similar sales should be enough to get the system selling for you, with Amazon recommending your book via email or in various positions around the site where Amazon advertises books to readers.

Spreading The Love is the safest way to launch a book and should lead to more gradual sales that will see you far better off by the end of the month. That, in turn, leads to a smaller cliff, because the sales are spread out much more than the one-off spike you get from the conventional approach.

However, it may not appeal to gambling types who like to roll the dice a little more. They may prefer *Going For Broke.*

27. Going For Broke

I must stress at the outset that *Going For Broke* is a much riskier strategy. But if you have multiple titles coming out and don't mind writing one off as an experiment, or if you have a book that's only going to be published for a limited time or a title that is particularly time sensitive, then this approach could suit you.

One example might be a short story collection for Christmas or Halloween. Such titles might be unlikely to sell much outside of a certain time of year, so you might want to goose sales as much as possible in the small window you have. Another example might be a box set. As a series writer, you may decide to compile the entire series to sell it as a box set for a limited time. Often, box sets are only available briefly because series writers prefer readers to buy each book individually. They make more money if readers buy the books separately, and having both a box set and the individual books out can dilute your sales between the titles, which will, in turn, adversely affect potential chart placement and associated visibility. However, making box sets available for a brief period can be a nice way to make some extra money on a series that has been flagging. Once the sales wave subsides, you can pull the box set and refocus your promotional energy on the individual books.

In both cases (seasonal releases and box sets), you may consider it advantageous to take a more aggressive approach to launching your book, as the window for selling has been truncated. You don't need to keep any promo bullets in your gun, and you can wheel out every trick in the book over a short space of time. For all other titles, please be aware that once you use this approach to launch a book, you have fewer options to remedy flagging sales in the months afterward.

The Nitty Gritty

The basic aim of this strategy is to pin your book to the top of the Popularity Lists for your chosen categories right from the start, and then to hope that such top-level visibility is self-sustaining. It will only work if you are in relatively large categories (apologies to authors of Cat Sleuth Mysteries!), and, as flagged, it's a bit of a gamble.

The way it works is simple... on paper. Instead of holding back the usual tricks for boosting sales further down the road, you put everything on the line straight away to maximize your 30-day average as soon as possible.

As explained in *Chapter 8,* the Popularity list is calculated on a rolling 30-day average. However, if your book has only been out for a week, your average is calculated across that week rather than across 30 days. A strong opening week can give you a significant leg up. But strong sales might not be good enough.

To deploy this strategy effectively, you need some serious promotional firepower. You need to open with a price no prospective purchaser can refuse: 99c. You need to combine that "impulse-buy" price with as many promotional fireworks as you can muster: a group promotion; an ad or selection of ads with large reader sites such as BookBub, ENT or POI; and, if possible, a guest post on a *major* blog or review site.

Please note that many reader sites will only take an ad for a book that already has a certain number of reviews, and for a book that has already been released. However, if you have a track record of good performance, they may waive that prerequisite. If the book is a box set and the books it contains have already done well, this could be another way around the minimum review requirement.

The aim is to maximize sales in those opening few days. If these kind of large-scale promotional opportunities aren't available to you during launch week, this strategy is *not recommended* (but the next strategy—*Seeding With Freeloaders*—could work for you).

28. Seeding With Freeloaders

This strategy is a variation on *Going For Broke* and the same caveats apply: it's a risky approach that is probably more suited to books with a limited sales window (like seasonal anthologies and recipe books, or box sets that are only available temporarily).

Going For Broke is essentially an attempt to seed the Popularity lists in your categories. This strategy is similar, except you're aiming to boost your Popularity list placement with free downloads. For this to work, your book needs to be in KDP Select, you have to have a good relationship with the big reader sites (i.e. sites such as Pixel of Ink and Ereader News Today regularly feature your free books), and you have to be willing to spend a small amount on an ad or two. You will also be sacrificing all mailing list sales and offering them a free download instead, which may be significant lost income.

In short, *Seeding With Freeloaders* requires that when you release your book, you do a free run via KDP Select straight away, announcing it to your mailing list and social networks as a special treat, racking up thousands of downloads, waiting for the book to return to the paid listings, and then enjoying the bounce up the rankings caused by improved Popularity List placement. To further boost downloads in the required period, a BookBub ad is strongly recommended, and you should seek to be featured on whatever reader sites you can. Be warned that many of the reader sites (including BookBub) may hesitate about featuring a new release, particularly if it doesn't have many reviews. You can attempt to combat this by providing advance reader copies to reviewers, but be warned that you may face difficulty purchasing ads.

The dangers of this strategy should be clear. You would be sacrificing guaranteed sales from your mailing list and platform with no guarantee of a return. Even with thousands of downloads, the post-free bump might be negligible. If you have no mailing list to speak of and little in the way of platform, then the potential reward might be worth the risk. But, to be clear, I'm not recommending either *Going For Broke* or *Seeding With Freeloaders* as a launch strategy for most books or authors. *Spreading The Love* is (by far) the most dependable approach, and is usually very effective too.

I'm presenting the alternative strategies for a couple of reasons. First, as explained, certain categories of books require a big push in a limited time frame. Second, experienced self-publishers with multiple titles, and who produce new work quickly and regularly, might feel that they can take a gamble with one of the riskier strategies.

The rewards can be great, but there is real risk here. If the launch doesn't come off as planned (and success is far from guaranteed), you face an uphill battle to get that book off the ground, and you can't seek help from the usual sources because you have already tapped them. Keep that in mind, and choose carefully.

PART VI: SELLING OUTSIDE OF AMAZON

In this final section, we leave the sanctity of Amazon to take a look at the other retailers, which make up about a third of the market in the US and a tenth in the UK. You'll find out why self-publishers don't tend to do as well outside of Amazon, except in certain genres, and you'll discover the strategies that are employed by the minority of self-publishers who buck that trend.

29. Challenges

Barnes & Noble seems to have taken some of its bricks-and-mortar mindset online, because through accident or design, opportunities for visibility on the Barnes & Noble site are scarce. Unlike Amazon, where many of the places where books are recommended to readers are up for grabs in a kind of convoluted meritocracy, on retailers such as Barnes & Noble, Apple, and Kobo those spots are virtual co-op, either parceled up and sold off to large publishers or hand-picked books chosen by merchandizing teams. Naturally, this makes gaining traction extremely difficult.

Other paths are also closed off to the self-published author seeking to gain momentum. There are no Top Rated lists on Barnes & Noble or Kobo, so you won't be able to put your book front and center on the strength of reader reviews alone. The big site promos for those two retailers tend to only include books from major publishers. Search functionality is poor on both sites too (and it's particularly bad on Kobo). Categories are a mess. All of this, again by accident or design, serves to focus sales on the Best Seller lists and the books sold by large publishers, which are either handpicked for promotions or sold into co-op spots.

On Amazon, a book can find its feet over time. It can start off in a smaller category before gaining traction and moving up the various lists until it is ready to compete in a larger category. There are multiple paths to the top, all of which feed into each other and amplify a book's progress. A well-executed free run can lead to a spate of borrows, which can turn into a run at the top of the charts.

The other retailers have fewer lists, making it harder for a book to fight its way up. If you can't make a big splash quite quickly, you're pretty much invisible. It's easier in some genres than others. And it is easier with certain kinds of books than others. But there are ways to make that splash.

30. Strategies for Success

Barnes & Noble, Apple, and Kobo all have less churn on their Best Seller lists. There are multiple reasons for that, but the main factors are the way their algorithms treat historical sales, and the simple matter of fewer paths to the top and thus fewer books pushing you down every day. While this makes cracking the Best Seller lists tricky, it also means that if you are successful, your ranking doesn't decay as quickly, which, in turn, means you tend to hang on to chart position a little longer and stretch out sales for a more sustained period after any spike. In short, it means most strategies for success are, out of necessity, big and bold. Here are a variety of methods self-publishers use to boost sales outside of Amazon.

The Right Genre

Romance and erotica writers can do exceptionally well on Barnes & Noble (even though both categories are affected by a rumored policy of front-loading 1000 ranks on any erotica or 99c titles that break into the Top

100, unceremoniously removing them from the charts). Fantasy and science fiction authors are reportedly making inroads on Apple, where authors of illustrated books and graphic novels have also been seeing some success. Switching genres may not be an option (or wise), but for those who write in multiple genres, it's something to consider.

Perma-Free

The process of making a book perma-free was explained in *Chapter 12: Free Matching*. It basically involves making a book free on Smashwords, Kobo, Apple, and Barnes & Noble, and then waiting for Amazon to match that free "price." The audience-building effect of this strategy is clear and proven, and is one of the few ways self-publishers are able to proactively build a readership outside of Amazon (rather than hoping for luck to strike or for word-of-mouth to do its thing). Authors such as Lindsay Buroker, David Dalglish, Monique Martin, and Sarah Woodbury have built significant readerships outside of Amazon by making the first book in a series free, permanently, everywhere. For standalone titles, free pulsing is a great approach outside Amazon too.

BookBub

Most of the reader sites, big and small, focus exclusively on promoting books on Amazon due to its lucrative and extensive affiliate program. BookBub is one of the few that permits links to all sites, and the only one with significant reach, especially on Barnes & Noble. As flagged in *Chapter 20: The Major Sites*, BookBub ads don't come cheap, but the ability to really jumpstart sales on Barnes & Noble and Apple (results aren't as impressive on Kobo), factored with the slower decay of those sales versus Amazon sales, might just tip the scales for you.

Patience

Aside from a BookBub boost, the consensus is that success outside of Amazon is a slower build. If you are pulling titles out of KDP Select one month, impatiently watching sales for a couple of weeks, and then contemplating granting Amazon exclusivity once more, you haven't given yourself a chance. Any hard-won momentum will be lost, and by the time you do return to all retailers, any readers you may have gained will probably have forgotten about you. Building an audience outside of Amazon takes time, but remember that having only one income stream leaves you vulnerable to a sudden dip or a change in policy.

Waiting can be a slow, frustrating process, but if you can be patient and boost sales where possible with judicious use of sales, free runs, and advertising, you increase your chances of success. There are a lot of readers on the other retailers, and they don't get as large a selection of bargain and free books. If you can tap into that, you have a shot.

32. Amazon & Exclusivity

After reading this section, you may have already decided to enroll your books in KDP Select (or keep them there), especially if you have largely stand-alone titles or you only write in certain genres. However, some of you may still be unsure. This chapter will look at the pros and cons from all angles.

Benefits

Enrolling in KDP Select gives your book measurable benefits. For starters, that title is made available in the Kindle Owners' Lending Library, from which any Amazon Prime subscribers can borrow one book a month. Aside from receiving compensation for those borrows (which is usually around $2), each borrow counts as a sale in the calculations made to determine Sales Rank.

You also get additional exposure in the KOLL charts. As explained in *Part I: Amazon Algorithms*, the KOLL charts are essentially the Popularity lists with non-eligible books removed. As those non-eligible books include almost all of the books from large publishers and anything from a small publisher or self-publisher whose books aren't enrolled in KDP Select, it is much easier to gain traction on the KOLL charts. A sales spike or free run can catapult your book to the upper reaches of the KOLL charts, leading to further borrows, and thus, further gains on the other charts.

Aside from borrows, enrolling in KDP Select allows you to efficiently manage free runs. As explained in *Part II: Free Pulsing*, attempting to go free via price matching is quite difficult to pull off, and much can go wrong. A KDP Select free run is the only way to guarantee the day that your book will go free, and when it will return to the paid listings. Having control over that is essential for maximizing the post-free bounce.

That bounce, as you should know by now, is caused by improved placement on the Popularity lists (where free downloads are counted as one-tenth of a sale). That new visibility leads to a spike in paid sales, which in turn improves your Sales Rank and position on all the Best Seller lists that you qualify for.

Costs

There are plenty of philosophical objections to KDP Select, some of which I share; most are to do with the exclusivity clause, with handing too much power to one retailer, and with the precedent it sets regarding author compensation under subscription models. However, I would like to focus here on the *practical* costs of enrolling a title.

The costs of enrolling in KDP Select are not easily quantifiable, not unless you already have a sizable readership outside of Amazon. If that is the case, you may have decided not to enroll your existing titles because of the exclusivity requirement. When you enroll a title in KDP Select, you must not publish a digital version anywhere else for the duration of your term (which is 90 days). Obviously, if you already have that title on other retailers, you must unpublish it. Doing so will cost you any (extremely hard-won) momentum you might have on those sites. When you do eventually return to those retailers, you will be essentially starting from scratch (although on some retailers your books may retain reviews).

Additionally, readers who frequent those stores may become annoyed at not being able to purchase your books. There's a good chance that they won't appreciate the rigmarole of purchasing from Amazon and converting to the kind of file they can use (and that's if they know how to do that), and there is a reasonable chance that they will have forgotten who you are by the time you exit KDP Select. It must also be remembered that because success outside of Amazon is such a slow build, you might not have even come close to exploiting your sales potential on other retail sites yet.

Summary

Philosophical objections aside, there are real costs to

enrolling in KDP Select, but there are real benefits too. While there is no one-size-fits-all answer, there's no denying that certain kinds of books and certain genres tend to outperform others outside of Amazon. If you are, for example, a series writer of historical romance, it's certainly worth exploring all sales channels. On the other hand, if most of your sales come from the UK, you might lose very little by granting Amazon exclusivity, as Amazon enjoys 90% of the ebook market in the UK.

For most authors, however, it won't be quite so clear-cut. You might have a small percentage of sales outside Amazon, but no real idea where your title might be in six months with a new release or two. You might also be wondering how substantially you could grow your Amazon sales with the promotional tools and extra visibility opportunities available to books enrolled in KDP Select.

You should make the decision on a book-by-book basis, and review it regularly. Some authors enroll all of their titles in KDP Select on release and then decide whether to widen their distribution based on that first 90-day term. If they get a lot of borrows, or have a successful free run, they tend to re-enroll for a further 90 days. Conversely, if it's the kind of book that the big reader sites don't feature, or if borrows are negligible, they often upload to all the other retailers and see how they fare.

If you don't have a clear path to achieving

visibility outside Amazon, or it seems forever out of reach, no matter what you try, you should strongly consider experimenting with KDP Select to see what that could do for your sales. Savvy self-publishers are increasingly exiting KDP Select with a least *some* of their titles in order to test the waters outside Amazon, the general feeling being that it's now harder to generate a post-free bounce. But it must be said that it is certainly still possible to have a successful free run that results in a significant sales spike. Whatever you decide, remember that neither decision has to be permanent. If one route isn't profitable, try the other.

33. Keep Writing!

It is time for me to shuffle back to my writing cave and start working on something new, because if there's one thing that will ensure you get better results from any of the strategies I've mentioned, it's more titles.

Publishing more books helps in innumerable ways. You have more titles to experiment with, to advertise, or to make free. Each new title is an opportunity: both to sell that book and to promote everything else you have out. Each promotion creates spillover sales for your other titles. Each launch creates a trail of Internet breadcrumbs that lead back to you and your books. Each time you hit your mailing list, you remind existing readers that you are still creating. Each book reaches new readers who can spread the word to their friends. And each book is another opportunity for you to be discovered.

Frankly, a lot of this business is luck, but I believe you can increase your chances by being smart and working hard. Now that you understand how Amazon works, you can take advantage of that knowledge and schedule promotions that maximize your opportunities for visibility. Just knowing how the system works will help you act reflexively when crafting marketing plans and when evaluating promotional opportunities.

All of this may seem far removed from the idealized notion of a writer working away in a Parisian garret. This business can be crazy-making, but writers should never forget how lucky they are. Not only do we have powerful tools at our disposal to publish books and reach readers around the world, we also have it much easier than other artists.

My fiancé runs an art gallery in East London and I get to meet artists from all disciplines—photographers, painters, jewelers, sculptors—all doing the same thing as us, creating something and trying to interest people in it. It's incredibly difficult. I see amazing art all the time that barely registers with the outside world. Some of these guys are incredibly talented. And they labor away in the darkness, struggling, doubting, and, for the most part, failing.

A sculptor slaves away on a piece—a real object in the physical world—and can only exhibit it in one gallery at a time. Even if the sculptor is lucky and the right person discovers it (and purchases it), her piece can only be sold once. Then she must start the whole process over again, attempting to interest someone else in something new she has created.

Writers have it so much easier. These days, the books we make and sell are largely digital objects; we pay to make them just once and we then have the luxury of selling infinite copies. We can write about whatever we like, and we can sell it to whomever we like, over and over again. And we get to keep most of the money. What could be better than that?

I hope you found this book helpful. The ideas discussed here should help you get more exposure, but you will get more out of this approach with more titles on sale. Don't let marketing intrude on precious writing time, and keep your primary focus on producing quality new work.

Now go forth and get visible.

The Advanced Author Toolkit

This section provides a compendium of tools to help you in your mission to achieve visibility. I'm presuming you already own a Kindle. If you don't, you really should get one. Amazon is by far the largest market, and now that the price has dropped to $69/£69 for the most basic model, there really is no excuse. As for the rest of this stuff, don't worry. It's free (and some of it will even *make* you money).

Google Alerts

When your sales have a sudden, inexplicable spike, it's important to find out what the cause was. Maybe it was a new reader site that is gaining ground on the top dogs, or perhaps an influential book blogger reviewed your book. Setting up Google Alerts (*bit.ly/Visible32*) on your name and book titles will alert you to anything published online containing the terms you choose. You can set alerts to email you as-it-happens (or, to be more accurate, as the Google bots discover the page, which can be minutes or days later), daily, or weekly. I tend to opt for as-it-happens. Unless your book has a very generic title and/or you have a very common name or a name that is shared by a celebrity, you won't get too many emails.

Tracking Sales

Novelrank (*bit.ly/Visible33*) is a great tool for tracking book rankings. Its Sales Rank figures tend to be about an hour behind the real thing (it takes an API feed direct from Amazon), but can sometimes be slightly laggier. It doesn't automatically track books—you have to enter them into the system—but once somebody starts tracking a book, that title's details are viewable to all. It will also record the ranking continuously, so you can view the historical performance of tracked books.

Two things to note. First, if a book goes free, Novelrank will stop following it and you must reactivate the tracking. Second, ignore the sales estimates; they are completely off, and only tend to be accurate if a book is selling few copies a day, anything more than that and the system seems unable to estimate with any accuracy. However, the ranking estimates are *very* accurate, and you can extrapolate sales from that.

KND Tracker

While NovelRank is a good tool for checking ranks, if you really want to dig into historical ranking data, or get more detailed data about those ranks, KND Tracker (*bit.ly/Visible34*) is superior. It doesn't cover all of the international Amazon sites like NovelRank, but it makes up for it with handy features such as being able to batch together a group of titles to monitor their performance simultaneously.

Rank to Sales Estimator

I've reprinted this chart from *Chapter 1* purely for ease of reference:

#1 to #5 = 3,500+ books a day (sometimes a lot more).
#5 to #10 = 2,000–3,500 books a day.
#10 to #20 = 1,100–2,000+
#20 to #65 = 850–1,100
#80 = 850
#90 = 750
#275 = 325
#500 = 200
#1000 = 100
#2000 = 50–55
#3000 = 40–45
#4000 = 30
#5000 = 20–25
#7500 = 16
#12000 = 10
#25000 = 5
#32000 = 3
#42500 = 2
#70000 to #100000 = 1
#100,000+ = less than 1 a day.

Tracking Clicks

Bit.ly is a free URL-shortening device that allows you to track when and how often your links were clicked and shared through social media (and any other websites on which you place your links). Using Bit.ly is simple. You sign in with your Twitter account and paste the link in the highlighted box. It will then give you a unique, shortened version of that link for use on Twitter and elsewhere (which you can customize, if you prefer). The site will track all clicks made on that link over time, and you can view the stats over various time periods.

It is incredibly useful for seeing which links in your tweets were actually clicked on, and whether they were retweeted. You can also use it to track clicks on links placed on your blog and on Facebook. Over time, you can begin to see what kinds of tweets and posts most appeal to others and inspire clicks (usually on the link to your book's product page on Amazon or elsewhere) and tweak your tweeting practices accordingly. You can also tweet directly from the Bit.ly interface, which is very handy.

SmartURL is a similar service, and is also free, but it offers one extra, important feature. It determines the location of the person who is clicking on the link, and once set up, can automatically direct them to the appropriate Amazon sales site dependent on their IP address. This is especially handy for Amazon book links because you can direct readers to the UK, French, German, Italian, Spanish, or Japanese Kindle Store (if that's where those clicking the links are located). You can also set a default URL for users who haven't been specified a location; in that case, it might direct them to the US Kindle Store, which serves all of the countries that lack their own specific store. I should point out that if you don't add an affiliate code to Amazon links, SmartURL will insert their own, which means they will make money every time you use the service—money you could be earning instead.

Amazon Associates

Amazon run an affiliate scheme called Amazon Associates (*bit.ly/Visible35*) on both the US and UK sites (they also have a similar service on some of the other European sites, but using it requires filing laborious paperwork). In short, whenever your links bring a customer to the Amazon store, Amazon pays you a percentage of the sales that customer makes. Doing so can also provide you with crucial data that you can use to hone your marketing efforts.

First, the money. Percentages vary depending on the type of product, and increase when you bring more business Amazon's way. A key thing to note is that Amazon doesn't just pay affiliates based on what they link directly to, it pays a percentage of *anything* that customer purchases. Amazon tracks the customer's activity via cookies, so even if you bring them to the site and they just sample a book before purchasing the following day, you will still get a percentage of that sale.

You are allowed to link to your own books and earn commission on those sales too. I'm currently earning about 7% on e-book affiliate sales. In practice, this means that I earn 42c for the sale of a 99c book (instead of 35c), and $3.84 for my books priced at $4.99 (instead of $3.49). That might not sound like much, but each time I sell 1,000 copies of the latter, it means an extra $350 in my pocket. And with all the other items that people buy, I can earn substantial sums—enough to cover the cost of all of my marketing last year.

To turn a normal link into an affiliate link, you just need to add your affiliate code to the end of the URL of the product page you are linking to. You will get your own unique affiliate code when you sign up, but note that the codes are different for each country's affiliate program, and you must use the correct one when linking to the respective store.

To make affiliate links look a little less messy, you can also run them through URL-shortening services like Bit.ly and SmartURL and you will still get your affiliate commission. When you put affiliate links on your blog or website, you should put a note in the footer stating that you use affiliate links. Amazon suggests language along the lines of "This blog is a participant in the Amazon Services LLC Associates Program, an affiliate advertising program designed to provide a means for sites to earn advertising fees by linking to amazon.com."

It's important that you don't use affiliate links when submitting a book for review, or for an ad spot, or to be featured on a reader site. They will want to insert their own links: after all, affiliate income enables them to keep the lights on. Aside from that, feel free to use them when you can.

Okay, that's the money side of things. Now, on to the tracking. When you look at your affiliate report, you will see that Amazon tells you how many times your links were clicked, and what percentage of those clickers bought that product or purchased something else. This is crucial data that will help you shape your marketing efforts. If you notice, for example, that you have a particularly low conversion rate (the percentage of clicks that turn into purchases) on one of your titles, you might consider freshening up the blurb. You can view the reports by any date range you choose to measure the outcomes of any changes you make.

Advertising Freebies

The three main reader sites to notify about an upcoming freebie are Ereader News Today, Pixel of Ink, and Kindle Books & Tips (formerly Free Kindle Books & Tips). BookBub has more power than any of them to shift free books, but you have to pay for the privilege with Bookbub whereas the first three don't charge. As for the small-to-medium sites, things are in quite a bit of flux at the moment with Amazon changing their affiliate rules. Many sites have either started charging authors to feature their freebies, stopped featuring free books altogether, or have simply closed down. KBoards (formerly known as KindleBoards) is the best place to hear about new sites that are worth notifying about freebies (and to evaluate if any of them are worth the fees being charged).

Stop Wasting Time on Facebook!

One of the great things about the modern world is that we have the entire repository of human knowledge at our fingertips, and we can connect with anyone on the planet. But that's also a terrible thing for the typical easily distracted writer, who can lose hours following links on Wikipedia, or talking with friends on Twitter. Because I have zero willpower, I use a program called Freedom (*bit.ly/Visible36*) to block the Internet for set periods. It's $10, you can get it for PCs and Macs, and there's a 90-day money back guarantee. It is easily the best $10 I've ever spent. Mac owners also swear by a similar program from the same developers called Anti-Social (*bit.ly/Visible37*). It blocks social sites like Twitter or Facebook, as well as anything else you add to the list, but leaves the rest of the internet open for regular research. It's $15, and Mac-only for now.

Now you should have all the tools you need to make your books visible *and* to switch off the noise and write more books. No more excuses. See you at the top of the charts!

Acknowledgements

The ideas in this book came from watching self-publishers a lot more successful than me, and then pestering them relentlessly. So many authors were generous with their time and their data, but a select few must be mentioned.

Debora Geary pretty much pioneered this approach, and put up with unending questions from me. Ed Robertson and Phoenix Sullivan delved deeper into the Amazon code than anyone else, then unselfishly shared their findings. Phoenix also gave excellent advice on an earlier draft, as did Monique Martin and Cidney Swanson. My blog readers gave great feedback on some of the ideas here. And a whole group of authors got together to pool sales numbers and figure out the algorithms. They know who they are, and they have my deep and abiding gratitude. There's no way I could have done this without them.

I must also thank my production team, editor Karin Cox, cover designer Kate Gaughran, and print formatter Heather Adkins, who had to put up with missed deadlines and moving goalposts, yet did sterling work. Finally, to Ivča: we'll get there, promise.

About the Author

David Gaughran is an Irish writer, living in London, who spends most of his time traveling the world, collecting stories. He's also the author of *Let's Get Digital: How To Self-Publish, And Why You Should*, *A Storm Hits Valparaiso*, *If You Go Into The Woods*, and *Transfection*, which are available from all major e-bookstores. *Digital* and *Storm* are also available in paperback.

If you want to get an automatic email when David's next book is released, sign up at *bit.ly/dgmlist*. Your email address will never be shared and you can unsubscribe at any time.

Word-of-mouth is crucial for any author to succeed. If you enjoyed the book, please consider leaving an online review, even if it's only a line or two; it would make all the difference and would be very much appreciated.

Say Hello!

David talks about writing and the book business on his blog *Let's Get Digital*. He would love it if you dropped by to say hello. You can also pop by South Americana where he shares curious incidents from the history of the world's most exotic continent. Alternatively, you can follow him on Twitter, get in touch on Facebook, or send him an email.

Publishing blog: *davidgaughran.wordpress.com*
South Americana: *SouthAmericana.com*
Twitter: *twitter.com/DavidGaughran*
Facebook: *facebook.com/DavidGaughranWriter*
Email: *david.gaughran@gmail.com*

Made in the USA
Charleston, SC
12 December 2016